Socialization

Key Concepts Series

Barbara Adam, *Time*
Alan Aldridge, *Consumption*
Alan Aldridge, *The Market*
Jakob Arnoldi, *Risk*
Will Atkinson, *Class 2nd edition*
Colin Barnes and Geof Mercer, *Disability*
Darin Barney, *The Network Society*
Mildred Blaxter, *Health 2nd edition*
Harriet Bradley, *Gender 2nd edition*
Harry Brighouse, *Justice*
Mónica Brito Vieira and David Runciman, *Representation*
Steve Bruce, *Fundamentalism 2nd edition*
Joan Busfield, *Mental Illness*
Damien Cahill and Martijn Konings, *Neoliberalism*
Margaret Canovan, *The People*
Andrew Jason Cohen, *Toleration*
Alejandro Colás, *Empire*
Patricia Hill Collins and Sirma Bilge, *Intersectionality 2nd edition*
Mary Daly, *Welfare*
Muriel Darmon, *Socialization*
Anthony Elliott, *Concepts of the Self 4th edition*
Steve Fenton, *Ethnicity 2nd edition*
Katrin Flikschuh, *Freedom*
Michael Freeman, *Human Rights 4th edition*
Russell Hardin, *Trust*
Anthony Heath and Yaojun Li, *Social Mobility*
Geoffrey Ingham, *Capitalism*
Fred Inglis, *Culture*
Robert H. Jackson, *Sovereignty*
Jennifer Jackson Preece, *Minority Rights*
Gill Jones, *Youth*
Paul Kelly, *Liberalism*
Anne Mette Kjær, *Governance*
Ruth Lister, *Poverty 2nd edition*
Jon Mandle, *Global Justice*
Vanessa May, *Families*
Cillian McBride, *Recognition*
Marius S. Ostrowski, *Ideology*
Anthony Payne and Nicola Phillips, *Development*
Judith Phillips, *Care*
Chris Phillipson, *Ageing*
Robert Reiner, *Crime*
Michael Saward, *Democracy*
William E. Scheuerman, *Civil Disobedience*
John Scott, *Power*
Timothy J. Sinclair, *Global Governance*
Anthony D. Smith, *Nationalism 2nd edition*
Joonmo Son, *Social Capital*
Deborah Stevenson, *The City*
Leslie Paul Thiele, *Sustainability 2nd edition*
Steven Peter Vallas, *Work*
Stuart White, *Equality*
Michael Wyness, *Childhood*

Socialization

Muriel Darmon

Translated by Lucy Garnier

polity

Copyright © Muriel Darmon 2024

The right of Muriel Darmon to be identified as Author of this Work has been asserted in accordance with the UK Copyright, Designs and Patents Act 1988.

First published in 2024 by Polity Press

Polity Press
65 Bridge Street
Cambridge CB2 1UR, UK

Polity Press
111 River Street
Hoboken, NJ 07030, USA

All rights reserved. Except for the quotation of short passages for the purpose of criticism and review, no part of this publication may be reproduced, stored in a retrieval system or transmitted, in any form or by any means, electronic, mechanical, photocopying, recording or otherwise, without the prior permission of the publisher.

ISBN-13: 978-1-5095-5368-6
ISBN-13: 978-1-5095-5369-3(pb)

A catalogue record for this book is available from the British Library.

Library of Congress Control Number: 2023934595

Typeset in 10.5 on 12pt Sabon
by Fakenham Prepress Solutions, Fakenham, Norfolk NR21 8NL
Printed and bound in Great Britain by TJ Books Ltd, Padstow, Cornwall

The publisher has used its best endeavours to ensure that the URLs for external websites referred to in this book are correct and active at the time of going to press. However, the publisher has no responsibility for the websites and can make no guarantee that a site will remain live or that the content is or will remain appropriate.

Every effort has been made to trace all copyright holders, but if any have been overlooked the publisher will be pleased to include any necessary credits in any subsequent reprint or edition.

For further information on Polity, visit our website:
politybooks.com

Contents

Detailed Contents vi
Acknowledgments x

Introduction 1

1. Building People I: The Strength of Primary Socialization 8
2. Building People II: The Plurality of Primary Socialization 53
3. Rebuilding People: The Varied Forms of Secondary Socialization 77
4. Studying People-Building: Socialization across the Life Course 106
5. Engaging with Challenges Old and New: Race, Gender, Children's Agency 136

Conclusion 170

Notes 174
References 176
Index 189

Detailed Contents

Acknowledgments	x
Introduction	1
Chapter 1. Building People I: The Strength of Primary Socialization	8
1. Socialization and education	9
1.1 Socialization as education	9
1.2 Education as hypnosis	10
1.3 Beyond hypnotism	13
1.4 Socialization as the non-conscious aspect of education	14
1.5 Incorporation as the non-conscious aspect of socialization	15
1.6 History as the unconscious aspect of socialization	18
1.7 The hysteresis of the products of family socialization	19
1.8 Categories of socialization	20
2. The initial "folds" of social structure	23
2.1 The weight of history	23
2.2 Class socialization	25
2.2.1 The explanatory nature of social background	26

2.2.2 The "power of the past"	28
2.2.3 Observing family socialization	29
2.2.4 Play and social class	32
2.2.5 Space and time	34
2.2.6 The class-based incorporation of Black masculinities	39
2.3 Gender socialization	44
2.3.1 Incorporating gender	44
2.3.2 Games, leisure, and sports	47

Chapter 2. Building People II: The Plurality of Primary Socialization   53

1. Plural influences	55
1.1 From plural socialization to the "plural actor"	56
1.2 The social conditions of socialization	58
2. Intra-familial heterogeneity	60
3. Variations in childcare arrangements	63
4. Childhood professionals and educational norms	64
5. The influence of peers and the cultural industries	66
6. School: a hub for primary socialization	69

Chapter 3. Rebuilding People: The Varied Forms of Secondary Socialization   77

1. Defining secondary socialization	78
1.1 Primary socialization: strength and affectivity	78
1.2 The bureaucratic worlds of secondary socialization	80
1.3 The relationship between primary and secondary socialization	82
2. How a doctor is made: a "historical" example of professional socialization	83
2.1 *The Student-Physician*: medical culture and anticipatory socialization	84
2.1.1 Learning to reconcile contradictory norms	85
2.1.2 Finalism and socialization by the reference group	86

2.2 *Boys in White*: student culture and socialization by situation   87
    2.2.1 The making of a physician: a research program   87
    2.2.2 The anti-functionalism of *Boys in White*   88
    2.2.3 "Perspectives" as the products of socialization   90
    2.2.4 Primary and secondary socialization   93
2.3 Two different conceptions of socialization   93

3. Diverse secondary socialization   95
   3.1 Other forms of professional socialization   95
   3.2 Other forms of secondary socialization   98
     3.2.1 Marital socialization   99
     3.2.2 Group socialization   100
     3.2.3 Political socialization   102

Chapter 4. Studying People-Building: Socialization across the Life Course   106

1. The agents of continuous socialization   107
   1.1 The central role of institutions and their limitations   108
     1.1.1 Total institutions   108
     1.1.2 A model for analyzing the socializing effects of institutions   109
   1.2 Processes beyond socialization?   113
     1.2.1 Events   113
     1.2.2 Individual effort   114

2. How continuous socialization functions   116
   2.1 Diverse modes and mechanisms   116
   2.2 Through body, speech, or writing?   117
   2.3 How processes of socialization "fit together"   120

3. Continuous socialization: products and effects   122
   3.1 Emotions, feelings, and cognition: beyond socialization?   123
     3.1.1 Continuous emotional socialization   123
     3.1.2 Continuous sensorial and cognitive socialization   126
   3.2 Socialization as both continuous and powerful?   128
     3.2.1 Reinforcement socialization   128

3.2.2 Conversion socialization	130
3.2.3 Transformative socialization	132

Chapter 5. Engaging with Challenges Old and New: Race, Gender, Children's Agency — 136

1. What is racial socialization?	136
1.1 Becoming aware of race (or not)	137
1.1.1 Socialization to race and racism	137
1.1.2 Socialization to dominant positions in the social space of race	142
1.2 Incorporating "race"	144
1.3 Dealing with the difficulties of this approach	152
2. Doing gender or being done by gender?	155
2.1 Moving away from gender socialization?	155
2.2 A social space of socialization to styles of masculinity and femininity	160
2.3 Are desires tastes that we acquire?	162
3. What about children's agency?	163

Conclusion   170

Notes	174
References	176
Index	189

Acknowledgments

I would first like to thank three people without whom *Socialization* would not exist: Magne Flemmen, who had the idea for this book as a result of the most serious case of Sociologica Francophilia Fever I've ever encountered; Polity's Jonathan Skerrett, who let a Mariah Carey quotation convince him that it was worth giving socialization another chance, and more seriously for his faith in the project and his crucial help in this endeavor to revive the concept; Lucy Garnier, for her extraordinary translation and editing work (to which I am now so accustomed it no longer comes as a surprise) and for all our discussions about words that are always also discussions about things.

I would like to extend my thanks to Polity's peer reviewers for their helpful, constructive remarks throughout the project. When the manuscript was still in its early stages, I presented an outline of its content at the NYU Sociology of Culture Workshop where I received much decisive input from the participants' engaged discussion. I am grateful to them and to the organizers Paul DiMaggio, Carly Knight, and last but definitely not least Iddo Tavory, with whom I have now enjoyed nearly fifteen years of sociological conversation. My thanks go also to Martine Court for sharing her vast bibliographical knowledge and for having thought through the challenges of racial socialization with me.

Finally, I am grateful to Armand Colin for transferring the rights to a book written in French on the same topic, as well as to the ERC-funded GENDHI project (see below) and the TEPSIS LabEx (ANR-11-LABX-0067, coordinated by the EHESS) for funding both the translation of *Socialization* and the necessary bibliographical research trip – on which note "Patience" and "Fortitude" also deserve a special mention for welcoming me into their den during that time.

This study is part of the Gender and Health Inequalities (GENDHI) project, ERC-2019-SyG. The project has received funding from the European Research Council (ERC) under the European Union's Horizon 2020 research and innovation program (grant agreement No. 856478).

Introduction

Let us follow Norbert Elias's suggestion and imagine Robinson Crusoe and Friday from Daniel Defoe's eponymous novel on their desert island: alone, deprived of any external markers of their place in society, stripped of the wealth, objects, friends, and relatives that both differentiate them and make them feel that difference. Are they not society-less men, generic humans destined to act in exactly the same way within the material constraints imposed by the island? And yet,

> Robinson Crusoe, too, bears the imprint of a particular society, a particular nation and class. Isolated from all relations to them as he is on his island, he behaves, wishes and plans by their standards, and thus exhibits different behaviors, wishes and plans to Friday, no matter how much the two adapt to each other by virtue of their new situation, and transform each other in order to come closer together. (Elias 1991: 27)

In order for a "particular society" to act upon the two men, it does not need to exist in material form on the island: they carry it *within them* as "the human constellation" in which they have lived and were raised.

Robinson, who was brought up in the English bourgeoisie, risks his life to obtain knives and forks from a sinking shipwreck, so necessary are they to him; the first piece of furniture he makes is a table that he considers indispensable for, as he puts it, "I could not write, or eat, or do several things with so much Pleasure without a Table" (Defoe 2007: 59); he displays the same horror in the face of Friday's cannibalism as the latter expresses for the salt Robinson sprinkles upon his food; he creates separate rooms within his tent, distinguishing between a terrace, a cellar, and a kitchen; he keeps a diary, because for him, as for the author of his adventures, human experience is defined by narrative; he regulates his time meticulously with moments devoted to working, going out, and resting, and his days follow the immutable rhythm set out by this schedule.

In his island-bound solitude, everything this society-less man does testifies to a society-based relationship to the world, to space, and to time that was instilled in him previously, that he "brought with him" to the island, and of which he cannot and does not wish to rid himself. The process that took place during his English childhood and teenage years and that produced this very particular Robinson is what we call "socialization."

In this sense, socialization refers to all the processes through which an individual is constructed – or alternatively "formed," "shaped," "fashioned," "manufactured," "conditioned" – by the local and global society in which they live; processes during which they acquire – or "learn," "internalize," "incorporate," "integrate" – socially situated ways of acting, thinking, and being. The simplest definition that can be given of socialization, which will also serve as a guiding thread throughout this book as we explore various theories and empirical studies on the topic, is the following: "the way society forms and transforms individuals." Arguably, this definition raises more problems than it solves and, in doing so, it points to some of the tasks facing analyses of socialization: the vague term "way" must be replaced with actual, concrete *processes* (how does socialization operate?), the abstract, over-arching term "society" must be replaced by *agents* of socialization ("who" or "what" is doing the socializing?), and the generic reference to the actions of socialization upon individuals must be replaced by the analysis of its specific *effects*, *products*, *contents*, and *results* (what does the socialized individual internalize?).

Introduction 3

As general and broad as it may seem, this definition nevertheless excludes several other approaches and reveals some of the choices made in this book in order to provide a coherent pathway for the reader, looking at socialization as a specific notion understood in a particular way. Socialization is not a "domain" of facts, like family or school for example, but rather a way of envisaging reality, a perspective to be constructed. For this reason, its definition varies considerably from one scientific discipline to another and even from one researcher to another within the same discipline, and the various meanings in circulation do not necessarily have much in common. Faced with such an omnipresent concept, used in so many different ways, it seemed to me preferable to provide a specific reading of the notion, rather than to give in to the temptation of trying to provide an exhaustive catalog of its iterations. Rather than summarizing what such a catalog might look like, then, let us look instead at the series of choices that have determined the analytical pathway through the field of socialization proposed in this book.

Durkheim once declared "as a sociologist, it is above all as a sociologist that I shall speak to you of education" (1956: 28). In the same vein, this book discusses *sociological approaches* to socialization, to the exclusion of the sometimes related analyses carried out in other fields such as cultural anthropology or developmental psychology. In sociology, our definition of socialization also sets aside approaches that view it as something that generates social ties, or approaches that establish a close link between socialization, sociability, and ways of "building society" as opposed to ways of "being built by society." I therefore exclude from my purview here the sociological tradition embodied in particular by Georg Simmel, in which the notion of socialization is used to refer to the things that "transform the mere aggregation of isolated individuals into specific forms of being with and for one another" (Simmel 1950: 41). Similarly, I take my distance from another related meaning, namely socialization as the process through which an individual becomes part of a group and interacts with it. This is also the usage of the term and its derivatives that we most commonly encounter in everyday language, for example when we refer to a "well-socialized child," meaning a sociable child, capable of interacting with others in an appropriate manner, or when we use the term "socializing" to refer to meeting and mingling with other people. Furthermore, this book's fundamental conception of socialization in some ways resembles, but in others is distinct from, functionalist approaches that focus on the idea that we learn irreversible social roles in childhood, just as it stands apart from approaches that consider the free deployment of agency to be the mark of socialization.

Certain additional principles have contributed to defining what is and is not addressed in this book. Considerable space is given to empirical studies, especially those that focus specifically on socialization rather than simply alluding to it, for I agree with Cookson and Persell when they argue that "too often there is a kind of scholarly lip service paid to socialization without demonstrating its processes" (1985: 20). Moreover, where possible I emphasize analyses that look at *processes* of socialization rather than theoretical debates on its general role (whether in terms of reproducing the social order or of creating social ties).

One could be forgiven for thinking that this long series of restrictions will result in a somewhat narrow topic of study; however, this would grossly underestimate the scope of society's action upon the individual. Throughout this book, we will see the countless, and sometimes unexpected, areas in which society exercises its influence upon us: the things we like and are good at, whether academically or culturally; our eating habits, sporting habits, and body shape; our senses, such as sight or smell; the way we experience and express our emotions; our political leanings and actions; our relationship to time and how we use that time at work or in our leisure activities; how we behave when faced with official institutions; how we learn and perform our jobs, what our professional ambitions are, and how we envisage our futures; what we fear and what we desire; and much more besides.

Socialization *forms* us, body and soul, but it also *transforms* us, and this dialectical relationship between the shaping and reshaping of the individual is at the heart of my approach. I emphasize the fact that socialization determines who we are and that its products become "embedded" within the individual and are able to resist the passing of time, but I also underline the fact that socialization processes continue throughout the life course. One question therefore emerges from this dual perspective: what is the relationship between these different processes of socialization and how do they fit together? Answering this question means considering, first, how they are interconnected synchronically, when several agents of socialization coexist at a given moment in time (for example during childhood, when parents, extended family, peers, professional educators, and generalized educational norms must all be taken into account), and, second, how they are interconnected diachronically, when varied socialization processes follow on from one another (for example, in the family, at school, at work, in political groups, etc.) and not only *form* but also *transform* the individual.

This book's analytical pathway through various theories about and studies of socialization follows the same temporal logic. Chapters 1 to 3 focus on "primary" then "secondary" socialization, Chapter 4 provides an analytical grid for studying socialization as a whole across the life course, and finally Chapter 5 examines some of the challenges facing this particular understanding of socialization. Following the order of the life cycle and in keeping with a common distinction in sociology, I distinguish between primary socialization (which, as we shall see, must be considered in the plural) and secondary socialization. In sociology, the primary/secondary distinction is understood in three main ways, although the meaning is often implicit and sociologists tend to use the terms as though they were self-evident. First, the distinction can be predicated on the *agent of* socialization in question: in this case, primary socialization refers to what takes place in the family and secondary socialization to what is done by other agents. As the first two chapters of this book will show, however, this is a difficult distinction to maintain once extra-familial agents are involved, alongside the family, during the early childhood years. Second, although this is rarer, the distinction can be based upon the results of socialization: in this case, primary socialization will refer to all the processes that instill in the individual "fundamental" knowledge and attitudes, and secondary socialization to all the processes through which the individual "adds" less fundamental elements. Aside from the fact this second understanding of the distinction is abstract and lacking in precision, it also presents the disadvantage of being rooted in normative definitions of what the products of socialization are supposed to be. Finally, the third way in which the opposition can be understood is in terms of the life course, with primary socialization relating to everything that takes place during childhood and adolescence, and secondary socialization to everything that takes place in adulthood. This is the definition I adopt in this book, although I will be using it flexibly given how hard it can be to establish and respect a clear, systematic break between these two periods and thus between the two types of socialization. We will see, for example, depending on the chapter, that formal education can either be an agent of primary socialization, when it reinforces or competes with family socialization, or an agent of secondary socialization, when it provides professional training. For the sociology of socialization, what matters is not so much drawing up a fixed, universal typology of moments and agents of socialization as closely analyzing the various processes that *make up* socialization and therefore the individual themselves. This then offers a way of obtaining the necessary tools to understand its formative action throughout the life course.

Finally, this analytical pathway will show not only the full scale of society's formative action upon the individual throughout their life, but also the value of this particular concept when it comes to understanding that action. The value of socialization as a concept is no longer considered self-evident today and proving its enduring worth may be more necessary than with other sociological notions. In the United States, for example, it has long been discredited and eclipsed by other approaches, unlike in France where it remained in active use – notably in the teaching and research of various followers of Bourdieu such as Chamboredon – and then made a highly visible return to sociology from the early 1990s onwards with the work of Lahire. Diverse criticisms have been leveled against the concept since the 1960s (Wrong 1961), emanating from many different positions in the social sciences. The main arguments contended it was too deterministic and failed to allow for individual agency or social change. Other, more recent charges have, on the contrary, condemned its inability to take into account social structure or power relations. Over recent years, however, a new consensus seems to be emerging that it is time to ask "whatever happened to socialization?" (Guhin et al. 2021), to "resurrect" the notion (Fillieule 2013), "breathe life into this particular dead horse" (James 2013: 4), and take it "out of purgatory" (Haegel 2020), in short to "return to our roots" and bring about a "resurgence" of the concept (Jenkins et al. 2021).

This book does exactly that, inviting the reader to suspend whatever negative connotations the term "socialization" might have for them so as to consider with an open mind what it can still bring to the table today and, in particular, the light it can shed on some of the most contemporary aspects of our social world, without ever losing sight of the ways in which older social logics persist and are reproduced. *Socialization* promotes what could be defined as a maximalist, practice-oriented, and deterministic conception of its key concept, which, while it does not explain everything about society, can always explain something of it in all areas of practice. Far from being a relic of the past, mentioned only for history's sake in introductory textbooks but now largely obsolete, socialization may well be exactly what sociology needs today to move forward: a notion able to describe and explain both the reproduction and the transformation of societies in action, via individuals who are defined by their positions in the social space of class, gender, and/or race; an empirically grounded notion that allows us to take into account the multiplicity of the "plural actor" and what that actor does, as well as what can account for it; a way of understanding both structure and agency, through a renewed deterministic lens that does not deny individual activity but instead explains it by combining a focus on situation and a focus on individual dispositions. All this means that socialization is a conceptual tool through which it is possible to understand how and why we act as we act, think as we think, and become what we are.

1
Building People I: The Strength of Primary Socialization

It is commonly held that the first years of life are crucial to forming an individual, and many scientific disciplines have advanced this idea, especially subfields in psychology and sociology. However, we take this so much for granted that we often forget to mention, if only in passing, the *causes* of the particular influence wielded by the childhood or even teenage years. Why does this particular period in life, and especially parental education, have such formative power?

In order to explain the strength of primary socialization, sociologists have provided different answers to this question: because children are *easily influenced* and initial experiences have considerable sway over them (Émile Durkheim, Norbert Elias); because children have a veritable *need*, at this point in their development, for the influence of those around them so as not, or no longer, to be animals (Norbert Elias); because, at this stage in their lives, socializing influences are *imposed* upon children who cannot choose their parents or their parents' actions upon them, but also because this constraint operates within an *affective* context that lends primary socialization its particular tone and effectiveness (Peter Berger and Thomas Luckmann); and, finally, because initial experiences become the *filters* through which individuals go on to perceive the outside world, "selecting" the events, people, and perceptions that do not call into question the person they have become as a result of those initial experiences

(Pierre Bourdieu). For all these reasons, the education that individuals receive in childhood can be said to have a profound effect in forming the people they become.

1. Socialization and education

"Socialization" and "education" are not, however, equivalent terms. Socialization is more than just the effect of educational practices, that is to say the actions specifically and explicitly undertaken by parents with a view to raising their children in a particular way, even though studying those actions is essential to its analysis. Socialization also involves implicit processes, and sociological approaches examining it differ according to the degree to which they emphasize its various components and its conscious or unconscious aspects.

1.1 Socialization as education

Some sociologists have foregrounded the fact that children's "education" is at once the core of family socialization and the most visible part of the process. As Durkheim put it at the beginning of the twentieth century, in two often-quoted passages from *Education and Sociology*: "Between the vague potentialities which constitute man at the moment of birth and the well-defined character that he must become in order to play a useful role in society the distance is, then, considerable. It is this distance that education has to make the child travel" (1956: 84–5). "Education is the influence exercised by adult generations on those that are not yet ready for social life. Its object is to arouse and develop in the child a certain number of physical, intellectual and moral states which are demanded of him by both the political society as a whole and the special milieu for which he is specifically destined" (71).

In these excerpts, Durkheim uses the term "education" to refer to the "actions" undertaken by parents (although he refers to "teachers and parents" indiscriminately and considers the actions of school and family together) with a clear, explicit, and methodical aim: "creating a new being in man," that is to say the "social being" (1956: 126). At first glance, then, it seems that for Durkheim children are constructed entirely as a result of conscious, effective educational practices deployed by adults with this specific aim in mind. Children's "education" and "socialization" are taken to be equivalent processes.

From Durkheim's perspective, the processes in question are oriented in a particular direction: the intention is for the child to take on the "useful role" demanded by "society as a whole" and particularly the "milieu for which he is [...] destined." From this point of view, then, if we extrapolate a little, there are good forms of socialization that prepare children "well" for this role, and others that could be considered "bad."

This normative conception of socialization, determining what qualifies as "good" socialization, can also be found among some of the functionalist sociologists influenced by Durkheim. From their point of view, societies ensure the reproduction of culture and social structure by having children internalize norms and values, first and foremost within the family. For functionalist sociology, such as that of Talcott Parsons, "socialization is critical for the maintenance of both social continuity and *social order*, as actors learn both to imitate and to identify with others, eventually learning their specific 'role-values and symbol-systems'" (Guhin et al. 2021: 3).

This conception of things also entails identifying the predefined contents of socialization, which can then be said to have "failed" when they are not internalized and to have "succeeded" when they are. Looked at this way, the starting point for the sociological study of socialization is not so much the process itself as the social structure thanks to which we can identify what will, or what should, be internalized. The next stage is then studying the educational process by analyzing the *means* through which these contents will be taken on board.

1.2 Education as hypnosis

Durkheim uses a striking metaphor to characterize the strength and scope of these "means" and to show that

The Strength of Primary Socialization 11

primary socialization shapes children in deep and lasting ways. He argues that the power of educational action can be compared to hypnotic suggestion:

> (1) The child is naturally in a state of passivity quite comparable to that in which the hypnotic subject is artificially placed. His mind yet contains only a small number of conceptions able to fight against those which are suggested to him; his will is still rudimentary. Therefore he is very suggestible. For the same reason, he is very susceptible to the force of example, very much inclined to imitation. (2) The ascendancy that the teacher naturally has over his pupil, because of the superiority of his experience and of his culture, will naturally give to his influence the efficacious force that he needs. (1956: 85–6)

With this metaphor, Durkheim outlines an educational situation clearly characterized by the total passivity and lack of consciousness of those being educated, and the equally all-encompassing activity and lucidity of those educating them. Children are almost like blank slates, upon which adults, thanks to their "natural authority," can write whatever content they like, as long as they "wish" to do so. This aspect of Durkheim's analysis may well make us smile given how at odds it is with our current conceptions of childhood and education. It is as though he were talking about indoctrinating children into a cult rather than about educating them, and his text seems to be trapped in an old-fashioned educational model that today seems to us both dangerous and obsolete.

However, our instinctive reaction to distance ourselves from this point of view, and perhaps even consider it with some measure of condescension ("we know better now!"), should not prevent us from perceiving the significance of Durkheim's metaphor. Although the comparison with hypnosis is extreme, it has the advantage of emphasizing a fundamental aspect of the primary socialization process: at no point do children have even the illusion of being able to choose their influences. These are all imposed upon them. As the sociologists Peter Berger and Thomas Luckmann underscore:

> [A]lthough the child is not simply passive in the process of his socialization, it is the adults who set the rules of the game. The child can play the game with enthusiasm or with sullen resistance. But, alas, there is no other game around. [...] Since the child has no choice in the selection of his significant others [i.e. the individuals who will be important in his primary socialization], his identification with them is quasi-automatic. For the same reason, his internalization of their particular reality is quasi-inevitable. The child does not internalize the world of his significant others as one of many possible worlds. He internalizes it as *the* world, the only existent and only conceivable world, the world *tout court*. (1991: 154)

Berger and Luckmann's game metaphor is certainly more pleasing than Durkheim's hypnosis analogy, but the fundamental process in question (a game that is completely constrained in its very principles) is not so different. When we refuse to see childhood socialization as a long series of constraints, we are perhaps confusing modern educational standards (the "softer" more "democratic" way in which we believe children should be raised today) and the description of what a socialization process actually is, given that its mechanisms are necessarily constraining even when the content is not presented as such. It is important, therefore, not to conflate educational norms with the consequences of socialization processes, which are the same now as they were in Durkheim's day: children are shaped by the global and local society in which they are raised. The hypnosis model combines the notion of strong conditioning with the idea that we forget all about that conditioning after the event ("when you wake up [from your childhood] you will have forgotten almost everything about these hypnosis sessions but, without necessarily knowing why, you will see the world this way rather than that way, you will like this food not that food, you will do this sport, enjoy this cultural activity, have this political preference, and not others"). For this reason, Durkheim's model is perhaps more relevant than it initially seems and the rest of this chapter will try to show how and why that is the case.

1.3 Beyond hypnotism

First of all, criticizing Durkheim for adopting an approach to socialization that is too mechanical means overlooking all the ways in which he himself qualifies that mechanism. While his theories do principally seem to establish the existence of a socialization process that is very similar to deliberate, defined education, they in fact also reveal certain limitations to such explicit processes, which can help us to understand how and why socialization cannot simply be conflated with education.

Regarding the two points just emphasized (the passivity and lack of consciousness of those being educated, on the one hand, and the activity and lucidity of educators on the other), it is upon the second that Durkheim places the most limitations. As his book progresses, he identifies a certain number of reasons that call into question the educator's hyperconsciousness and omnipotence, reasons linked to the fact that "society" is more powerful still than educators who are themselves subjected to social rules that restrict their actions. This tells us that it would be a mistake to take too literally his idea of the educator's "natural" authority. First of all, in every era, educational norms are imposed with the strength of social facts and they prescribe how each generation of educators will raise children. We shall come back to this in more detail in Chapter 2. Furthermore, since education "reproduces" society but does not create it, educators cannot create in children dispositions that they do not themselves have and have not acquired during their own education (Durkheim 2005: 240). Finally, Durkheim argues that the construction of a social being is far from limited to the effects of intentional acts undertaken with that in mind:

> If teachers and parents were more consistently aware that nothing can happen in the child's presence which does not leave some trace in him, that the form of his mind and of his character depends on these thousands of little unconscious influences that take place at every moment and to which we pay no attention because of their apparent insignificance, how much more would they watch their language and their behavior! (1956: 86)

14 Building People I

The actions of educators upon children are therefore constant:

> There is no period in social life, there is not, so to speak, even a moment in the day when the young generations are not in contact with their elders and when, therefore, they are not receiving from them some educational influence. For this influence does not make itself felt only in the very brief moments when parents or teachers are consciously, and by explicit teaching, communicating the results of their experience to those who come after them. There is an unconscious education that never ceases. By our example, by the words that we utter, by the actions that we perform, we constantly mold our children. (1956: 91)

In these excerpts, we can see a very different conception of socialization from the one that I initially presented: the socializing moments that influence children are extended to all child–adult interactions, rather than being circumscribed within explicitly educational moments; socialization is more often unintentional than it is intentional; socialization is a continuous, diffuse, almost invisible process "of influence," which is a very different thing indeed from the hypnotizer's methodical pedagogical activity. Socialization and education are thus already distinct in Durkheim's thinking and he can help us to understand that the influence of socialization is not limited to explicitly educational moments.

1.4 Socialization as the non-conscious aspect of education

Pierre Bourdieu's notion of *habitus* offers us a theory of this non-conscious dimension. Very briefly, habitus can be said to be "a system of structured, structuring dispositions" (1990: 52) that underpins the practices and viewpoints of an individual or a class of individuals. For the purposes of the present study of socialization, what is productive is considering that the sociogenesis of the habitus is a socialization process: the habitus is constituted through the incorporation[1] of social conditions and past experiences, particularly from childhood. During the process of primary socialization, social structures are transposed into the family and then inscribed in children's minds and bodies through their everyday life:

> Through the economic and social necessity that they bring to bear on the relatively autonomous world of the domestic economy and family relations, or more precisely, through the specifically familial manifestations of this external necessity (forms of the division of labour between the sexes, household objects, modes of consumption, parent-child relations, etc.), the structures characterizing a determinate class of conditions of existence produce the structures of the habitus, which in their turn are the basis of the perception and appreciation of all subsequent experiences. (Bourdieu 1990: 54)

Reading the theory of habitus as a theory of socialization offers a complementary approach to analyses focusing on the strength of primary socialization insofar as it emphasizes the unconscious aspects of both the socialization process and its effects.

1.5 Incorporation as the non-conscious aspect of socialization

The non-conscious aspect of socialization relates above all to its corporeal dimension. Socialization is an "incorporation" or a "somatization" of the structures of the social world in which the body is treated as a "memory pad" (Bourdieu 1990: 68; 2000: 141) on which situations of existence are written down, or, in other terms, as "an automaton that 'leads the mind unconsciously along with it'" (Bourdieu 1990: 68), thus both guiding and constraining conduct. Each family's material conditions, the parents' relationships to the world (which they have themselves incorporated), and children's initial experiences are all, in a sense, directly inscribed upon and within their bodies without involving their "consciousness." As Bourdieu puts it, "the most serious social injunctions are addressed not to the intellect but to the body" and "we learn bodily" (2000: 141.) In the Kabyle house he studies as an example, children learn to "read the world" within the "space of objects" surrounding them, but this is a book that is "read with the whole body," through "movements and displacements" (Bourdieu 1990: 76). The internalization of the external, which produces the habitus, is therefore an incorporation (rather than an understanding or an interpretation) of the social world.

This imperceptible learning process shapes each body (and thus each individual) according to the structures of the milieu in which they grow up. Marcel Mauss, one of the pioneers of the sociology of incorporation, noted this as early as 1934 a propos some vivid examples: depending on the country, the military, and even civilians, do not walk in the same way, and people also do not swim in the same way depending on their generation. Regarding the latter example, Mauss explained that he could not help swimming by swallowing water and spitting it out again like a "steam-boat" because "in his day" this was how one learned to swim and his body knew no other way (Mauss 1973: 71).

From this perspective, socialization is not simply about internalizing the social world, less still about compiling available resources that one can decide to use or not. Socialization inscribes tendencies, reflexes, possibilities, and impossibilities deeply in the body. Even language, which is so intellectual and in some ways so immaterial, can reveal the weight of the body and its relative irreversibility in learning processes, as Dieter Vandebroeck reminds us:

> The difficulty that the average Anglophone speaker has in reproducing the speech pattern associated with the French "r" or that a French person has in pronouncing the English "h" provide a good example of the ways in which the early social conditioning of the body sets effective limits to its capacity to fully integrate new sensori-motor-habits [...] If, as every aspiring petit-bourgeois knows all too well, it is often much easier to change the grammaticality of one's speech act than it is to change one's accent, this is because "what is 'learned by body' is not something that one has, like knowledge that can be brandished, but something that one is." (Bourdieu 1990: 73) (Vandebroeck 2017: 45–6)

Socialization is incorporation insofar as it fashions bodies and bodies that are different. Bourdieu's work helps us to understand that, in doing so, it also fashions a relationship to the social world. For example, the instruction addressed to children to "stand up straight" is not just corporeal, it also contains the seeds for internalizing an ascetic relationship to the body and the importance of self-presentation, whilst bringing into play a moral contrast between good and slack posture, between controlled and lax behavior. We do not only incorporate that which is corporeal: categories of thinking, "cognitive structures," "schemes of perception and appreciation," "principles of division" (what is judged as "good" or "bad") – in short, everything that constitutes the lens through which we envisage the social world – are also "incorporated" during the socialization process, and are ready and waiting to be activated by situations and experiences.

It is in this respect that it is possible to talk about the "incorporation" of a form of capital as immaterial as "cultural capital," that is to say cultural heritage passed on from parents to children. Here again it is very clear how primary socialization can be distinguished from conscious, deliberate education. We know, for example, that when stories are read aloud to children, they are more likely to become readers themselves and that in some milieus this is a perfectly conscious educational strategy. However, a large part of cultural heritage is also passed on

> more discreetly and more indirectly, and even in the absence of any methodical effort or overt action. It is perhaps in the most "cultivated" backgrounds that there is least need to preach devotion to culture or deliberately to undertake initiation into cultural practices. [...] [T]he cultivated classes contrive diffuse incitements that are much more likely to induce espousal of culture through assorted hidden persuasion. (Bourdieu and Passeron 1979: 20)

This "hidden persuasion" can also be credited with the fact that cultural goods – for example, paintings, books, music CDs, "and particularly all those which belong to the childhood environment" – have an educational effect, if not "by their mere existence" then at least by their existence in combination with the way in which they are used by the adults surrounding the child (Bourdieu 1986: 27).

The fact that incorporation is not solely limited to the corporeal also means that there is something "all-encompassing" about socialization, because the incorporation of categories or attitudes based on a particular practical domain (how to hold one's body in public, for example, to return to the example of "stand-up-straight") can have effects and be activated in other practical domains (the relationship to others, the private/public divide, moral attitudes, and so on). This is what is referred to as the "transferability" or "transposability" of the products of socialization. Bourdieu refers to habitus as "systems of durable, transposable dispositions" (1990: 53). Dispositions – that is to say ways of being or doing, ways of seeing the world, tastes and distastes, the inclination to act in one way or another – are all internalized based on a given area of practice or a specific instance of socialization, but they can also have effects in other areas of practice or other social situations.

1.6 History as the unconscious aspect of socialization

In addition to the lack of awareness involved in the incorporation process itself, there is also a lack of awareness about its effects, that is to say the way in which it is "activated" in situations that can be very different from those in which the dispositions were originally instilled. We do not realize that we are "incorporating" things but we also don't always realize that, when we act, we do so because of what we have become as a result of this incorporation acting within us. As Durkheim already put it:

> in each one of us, in differing degrees, is contained the person we were yesterday, and indeed in the nature of things it is even true that our past personae predominate, since the present is necessarily insignificant when compared with the long period of the past because of which we have emerged in the form we have today. It is just that we don't directly feel the influence of these past selves precisely because they are so deeply rooted within us. They constitute the unconscious part of ourselves. (1977: 11)

The Strength of Primary Socialization 19

Bourdieu therefore positions himself within this same school of thought when he writes that the unconscious "is never anything other than the forgetting of history which history itself produces" and when he defines the habitus as "embodied history, internalized as a second nature and so forgotten as history [...], the active presence of the whole past of which it is the product" (1990: 56). When we come to look at class and gender socialization later, we will see some specific examples of this "embodied" or rather "incorporated" history that sometimes leads us to act without us necessarily being aware of it.

1.7 The hysteresis of the products of family socialization

According to the theory of habitus, primary socialization in the family also results in particularly stable products that are resistant to transformation. Bourdieu refers to the "hysteresis" of habitus that is constituted during family socialization, borrowing the term from physics where it refers to a lag between cause and effect, and a phenomenon that continues after its cause has disappeared. By extension, it is used in this context to describe the inertia of acquired dispositions, the resistance to change, and the individual's tendency to persist in the direction taken by family socialization:

> Early experiences have particular weight because the habitus tends to ensure its own constancy and its defence against change through the selection it makes within new information by rejecting information capable of calling into question its accumulated information, if exposed to it accidentally or by force, and especially by avoiding exposure to such information [and favoring] experiences likely to reinforce it. (Bourdieu 1990: 61–2)

This process selecting the places one goes to and the places one avoids, the events that matter and those one knows nothing about, the people who can be frequented and those to be avoided, is continuous, almost invisible, and often takes place beneath the level of conscious decision-making. It tends to protect the habitus from crises. Depending on the case, this kind of process can be particularly imperceptible because it relates to people's conditions of existence (for example, the spatial segregation that tends to group together similar individuals), or, on the contrary, it can be more conscious and deliberate, relating to educational strategies (for example, parents' desires for their children to avoid "bad company" and "unsuitable books") (1990: 61).

Family socialization therefore produces "irreversible dispositions," if by that term we mean not a definitive disposition but rather "a disposition which cannot itself be repressed or transformed except by an irreversible process producing in turn a new irreversible disposition" (Bourdieu and Passeron 1990: 42). From this perspective, it is therefore possible for the dispositions acquired during family socialization to be "repressed" or "transformed." But such a transformation requires very particular conditions capable of countering the hysteresis of family socialization. It is all the more improbable and difficult since any new process of socialization must allow for the results of primary socialization, i.e. what it has made of the individual. Primary socialization, "which is carried out by [pedagogical work] without any antecedent produces a primary habitus [...] which is the basis for the subsequent formation of any other habitus" (42).

For example, the habitus acquired in the family determines how school education will be received and assimilated. Certain types of family socialization will be more in line with the principles of school socialization than others: the upbringing of children from the cultivated middle and upper classes provides them with skills and tastes that correspond to those required by school. Differences between types of family socialization must therefore be seen for what they are – not just variations from one family to the next but a breeding ground for inequalities. This conjunction of the question of socialization and that of domination (whether relating to class or gender) leads us to the third main characteristic of family socialization: the fact that it includes different categories of socialization.

1.8 Categories of socialization

While Durkheim had already mentioned the social variability of education according to era, caste, class, and even gender,

Bourdieu systematized this approach and made social variability the main angle through which to analyze habitus. There are different categories of socialization and these produce different categories of habitus, and first and foremost class socialization and habitus. Because social class operates as "a class of identical or similar conditions of existence and conditionings," it is effectively "at the same time a class of biological individuals having the same habitus, understood as a system of dispositions common to all products of the same conditionings." Belonging to a given social class therefore results in forms of socialization that are if not identical then at least more similar than those found in other social classes:

> Though it is impossible for all (or even two) members of the same class to have had the same experiences, in the same order, it is certain that each member of the same class is more likely than any member of another class to have been confronted with the situations most frequent for members of that class. (Bourdieu 1990: 59–60)

This brings us back to the idea that socialization is made up of experiences that are then incorporated. The order in which they occur is also essential to understanding the process, because the incorporation of one experience will be part of the filter for the next one. Additionally, there is the fact that forms of socialization can be classified according to categories of class socialization. Class socialization comes from particular positions in the social space as analyzed by Bourdieu. To summarize simply, for the purposes of this book, the relevant points of a more complex theory, there are, according to Bourdieu, three types of capital that define an individual's social position. These are: economic capital (financial resources), social capital (personal networks and relationships), and cultural capital (cultural heritage, knowledge, and approaches to knowledge, typically measured by level of education). Bourdieu places particular emphasis on cultural capital in his approach to social hierarchies. In his analytical framework, an individual's position in the social space is defined by the overall volume of the capital they possess, which distinguishes the dominant class from the dominated classes. An individual's position is also defined by the structure of that capital (the respective amounts of economic and cultural capital they hold) that creates different "class fractions" differentiating those who possess relatively more cultural capital from those who possess relatively more economic capital. These different positions, in terms of both class and class fractions, produce different forms of class socialization, in terms of both processes and products.

In his book *Distinction*, Bourdieu offers an empirical demonstration of the effects of class socialization upon individuals' practices (what their socialization makes them do) and tastes and judgments (what their socialization makes them like, prefer, or hate, what it makes them value or stigmatize in others). Summing up this approach in *Practical Reason*, he writes:

> what the worker eats, and especially the way he eats it, the sport he practices and the way he practices it, his political opinions and the way he expresses them are systematically different from the industrial owner's corresponding activities. But habitus are also classificatory schemes, principles of classification, principles of vision and division, different tastes. They make distinctions between what is good and what is bad, between what is right and what is wrong, between what is distinguished and what is vulgar, and so forth, but the distinctions are not identical. Thus, for instance, the same behavior or even the same good can appear distinguished to one person, pretentious to someone else, and cheap or showy to yet another. (1998: 8)

By producing class habitus, class socialization therefore produces both objectively classifiable practices and systems for classifying them.

The existence of these class habitus does not, however, mean that individuals from the same social class are interchangeable and constitute social "clones." In Bourdieu's theory there are also "individual habitus" that constitute diverse singularities within the homogeneity produced by class habitus (Bourdieu 1990: 60). The specific contribution made by the theory of habitus lies, however, in the way it forces us to take into account something beyond the individual or the specificity of the family interactions that make up socialization, in order to understand the genesis of a given person. Looking *outside* the family – looking at the broader social structures in which it is embedded, that is to say considering that what happens in the family does not just depend upon the family – is perhaps the best way of understanding the socialization that takes place *inside* it.

2. The initial "folds" of social structure

This chapter will focus on three major types of conditions of existence and their effects, insofar as they represent three major principles according to which socialization varies. To summarize very briefly, family socialization does not produce the same person when one is born in the nineteenth century or the twentieth century, to a family of manual workers or senior managers, and as a girl or a boy. To use a metaphor coined by Gilles Deleuze and taken up by Bernard Lahire, these three principles of variation produce "folding operations" and an internalization of the social space within the make-up of an individual (Lahire 2011: 203–5). We can each be compared with a sheet of paper that has been folded up or a piece of fabric that has been crumpled as a result of the multiple "folds" of the social structure within us. What is "inside" (the individuality, categories of judgment, and tastes that we experience as personal) and what is "outside" (historical and social structures) are not in opposition, any more than a crumpled up piece of paper is in opposition with the same sheet of paper when it is unfolded.

2.1 The weight of history

According to Durkheim, in Ancient Rome, education aimed to produce Romans: each era marks its own specific characteristics in the generations raised within it and education "has varied [...] prodigiously in time and space" (1956: 120). While socialization is differentiated according to various factors (social class or gender, for example), it nevertheless produces a "common base" (119) that will oppose one generation to another and bring together those born at the same time. Durkheim cites the example of the Middle Ages, when "serfs, villeins, burgers and nobles received, equally, a common Christian education" (69), before going on to characterize what he considered the successive forms of education over the centuries – "ascetic in the Middle Ages, liberal in the Renaissance, literary in the seventeenth century, scientific in our time" (120). We can question the extent to which this "common base," which models all individuals of the same generation identically, truly exists. It is perhaps more productive to make a distinction, as Karl Mannheim does (1952), between different "generation units" coexisting within the same generational situation. However, Mannheim also advances the idea that belonging to a given generation unit does imply socialization effects that are common to different individuals, and that can therefore still be described as generational socialization.

For Norbert Elias, these educational models are part of an identifiable historical trend: socialization not only differs from one time period to another, it is in fact constantly progressing along an axis of increasing self-constraint. Elias's work makes a dual contribution to the analysis of socialization processes. First, because he examines the latter at the level of the individual and of the social mechanisms at work in childhood socialization, demonstrating how the sociological analysis of socialization can even account for something as exceptional as Mozart's musical genius (Elias 1993). Second, because he also examines how socialization processes evolve from the perspective of society as a whole, particularly in terms of their historical transformations. He analyzes "childhood socialization," the "formation of habits," and "conditioning" at the level both of personal and societal history. According to him, these two levels are connected by a "fundamental law of sociogenesis" (1994: 109). This law posits a homology between the trajectory of a child today during primary socialization and the trajectory of Western societies over the centuries:

> The history of a society is mirrored in the history of the individual within it. The individual must pass through anew, in abbreviated form, the civilizing process that society as a whole has passed through over many centuries;

for he does not come "civilized" into the world. (Elias 1994: 531)

This history is therefore the history of the progressive internalization of constraints. Elias highlights this process by studying books on manners, which have aimed, over the centuries, to educate children and adults. These books reveal "the standard of habits and behavior to which society at a given time sought to accustom individuals" and are effective instruments for the "conditioning" or "fashioning" of individuals by society (Elias 1994: 72). They demonstrate, among other things, the gradual shift from external constraint, coupled with conscious control exerted by individuals, to self-constraint functioning largely through automatisms. For example, just as today children progressively learn to use a fork because they are instructed to do so, or simply because they see adults doing it, and then come to consider this use necessary and to feel disgust at the idea of picking up certain types of food with their hands, so it is possible to retrace the civilizing process that gradually "introduced" the fork into our societies (first in some then in all groups) through explicit requirements (for example, books about manners) until this practice became an "automatic" need, without it even being necessary to impose it from one generation to the next. Elias also suggests extending this analysis to differences between nations, whose language, culture, and values fashion individuals who have similar characteristics (Noiriel 2003). Our current modes of socialization are therefore the "civilizational" product of both a given history and a given national context.

2.2 Class socialization

If an historical period constitutes a sort of common base for the socialization that takes place within it, it is therefore also a means of differentiation insofar as it opposes one generation to another. Within the same generation, however, another major differentiating factor between forms of socialization is children's social background, that is to say the class to which their parents belong. As the British sociologist Basil Bernstein has stressed, social class "deeply" marks forms of socialization:

The class structure influences work and educational roles and brings families into a special relationship with each other and deeply penetrates the structure of life experiences within the family. The class system has deeply marked the distribution of knowledge within society. It has given differential access to the sense that the world is permeable. It has sealed off communities from each other and has ranked these communities on a scale of invidious worth. (2003: 135)

2.2.1 The explanatory nature of social background

In a way, the idea that primary socialization produces effects is implicit in any statistical survey that considers social background (i.e. the respondents' parents' social position, not simply their own, even though the two are linked) as a factor explaining a given social practice. Studies on social mobility, which show how social background and social position are linked, are an obvious example and allow the hypothesis that when a practice can be explained by an individual's social position, their social background is perhaps also playing a role. Any study that highlights the differentiated effect of social class on practices or representations therefore reasserts the importance of primary socialization.

Where eating habits and their link with body weight are concerned, for example, these can also be explained in part by a person's class position.[2] The food people eat varies according to their social position and, for women at least, average body weight decreases the higher their social class. However, one can go further still and suggest that primary socialization (and its social class variations) plays an important role in establishing these differences, which can actually be described as inequalities whether in terms of public health or in terms of the symbolic benefits attached to possessing corporeal social excellence. Variations in rates of excess weight and obesity emerge at adolescence in both sexes: they are lowest among teenagers who have a parent who holds a managerial position or equivalent and highest among those whose parents are non-qualified workers. These variations reflect the social structure and are extremely likely to continue in adulthood. Different elements of socialization can help to explain how these "class bodies" are formed: eating habits (over-consumption of fatty foods with high calorie content, which are often cheaper, among the working classes compared to the upper classes; and, conversely, under-consumption of fresh fruit and vegetables, and unprocessed fish); sports habits (teenagers' sporting activities correlate with their parents' level of education; the higher their parents' qualifications, the more they engage in sports); patterns of bodily perception; "an ethic of convivial indulgence" (Bourdieu 1984: 179); and the hedonistic value of childhood in working-class families, which we will come back to later with Richard Hoggart's work. Therefore, as Dieter Vandebroeck has emphasized, class distinctions play a role in both the production and perception of weight differences, and Bourdieu's assertion that social actors are "classified by their classifications" can be taken *literally*. It is first of all partly through all of our routine tastes and practices (which are "practical classifications" that we make unconsciously) that our bodies are progressively *class*-ified, that is to say, acquire a distinct and characteristic social morphology. Moreover, our perceptions of our own bodies and of those of others are also embedded in the social space of class that determines these perceptions as well as whether we are dissatisfied or at ease with our bodies and whether we despise or admire those of others. These judgments (which sometimes become weight discrimination) can also be factors of symbolic violence. Rather than being perceived as purely "physical," weight difference is interpreted as providing an embodied indication of individual "personality" and moral "character." This allows distinctions to be drawn between the people whose physique testifies to their innate sense of self-control and determination and those whose bodies reflect "an inherent failure to transcend primal needs and desires, an intrinsic lack of self-control or self-respect and an abdication of personal responsibility, in short, [...] a culpable surrender to 'nature'" (Vandebroeck 2017: 82). Both the production and the perception of weight differences can therefore be at least partly traced back to family class socialization.

It is obviously difficult to observe this family class socialization in action, as it happens *and* throughout the whole time it happens. Ideally, in order to do so, one would have to spend several years continuously observing living conditions and parent–child interactions in the home, without this observation of private life altering the practices being observed. This does not mean, however, that sociologists are doomed to make hypotheses about socialization processes solely based on their results. Certain studies do provide access to important areas of this primary class socialization.

2.2.2 The "power of the past"

There are ways of highlighting the differentiated effects of class socialization while only examining its products, and this is what Jessi Streib does in the study from which I have borrowed the title for this section (2015). Her inquiry into "cross-class" marriages between white-collar and blue-collar families shows dispositional class differences within couples that result from the weight of their pasts and are especially apparent in these "different-origin" marriages. Streib's methodology avoids some of the pitfalls common to studies that only rely on retrospective childhood narratives to piece together conditions of socialization. In her study, she also asked her respondents how they perceived their families-in-law and collated testimonies about their in-laws' tastes and practices. This therefore allowed her to gather material about her respondents' partners' conditions of socialization as well. Her results show that the spouses have very different "sensibilities" in a range of practical areas and that the differences are systematic and structured according to social background. These sensibilities – a term she uses as "a nontechnical way to refer to the dispositions that are part of the habitus" (2015: 247) – are thus the result of class socialization that constructed in her respondents "differences in sensibilities about how to spend money, attend to work, divide household labor, use time, display emotions, and raise children" (8).

The spouses who were born into professional white-collar families possessed "managerial" sensibilities: "they preferred to plan, deliberate, mull over, and organize their resources, their children, and their daily lives." Mike, for example, "wanted to spend money carefully, plan his career trajectory, establish a structured division of labor, schedule his time, and think about his emotions before expressing them." Conversely, their partners with blue-collar roots typically had what Streib refers to as "laissez-faire sensibilities": "They preferred to feel free from self-constraint. Rather than wanting to analyze, plan, or meticulously organize their lives, they preferred to go with the flow and live in the moment." Mike's wife Christie, for example,

> wanted to feel free from the constraints of money and schedules so she spent money without thinking, decided in the moment how to use her free time, and took charge of the housework without imposing a structured division of labor. She also expressed her emotions without processing them, and, at work, she preferred to keep her eyes open for new opportunities rather than planning her career trajectory. (Streib 2015: 8–10)

These differences in sensibilities, which can be related to the spouses' social backgrounds and their primary class socialization, seem to be partly unrelated to gender, despite the gendered nature of marriage as an institution (and the differences established by gender socialization between spouses of different sexes, as we shall see later). Studies such as this one therefore show both the power and the enduring nature of the class dispositions produced by primary socialization.

2.2.3 Observing family socialization

Another research strategy for understanding this class socialization in action consists in observing what happens in childhood or adolescence, in order to see how early products of socialization become crystallized and what daily practices progressively lead to these dispositions being incorporated.

When it comes to observing family class socialization in the United States, Annette Lareau's study (2011), first published in 2003, is a classic. Her analysis is based on observations of daily family life in twelve families with nine- to ten-year-old children. These observations were carried out by researchers who asked to be treated "like the family dog," that is to say to be stepped over and mostly ignored, especially after a while, but to nevertheless be able to "hang out with" the family and therefore have direct access to extremely rich material on the socialization in progress. Lareau's analysis revealed the very strong social class variations between the different families she observed. Socialization processes in middle-class families were of the order of what she labels "concerted cultivation." Discussions were "a hallmark of middle-class child rearing," with children learning a certain type of language use, as well as the possibility and importance of reasoning and negotiating with adults. "Organized activities, established and controlled by mothers and fathers" were strongly prevalent and parents sought to "develop" their children in order to "cultivate [their] talent in a concerted fashion." These particular socialization processes produced a "robust sense of entitlement" in these children, which was evident in their relationships to adults (the children learned to challenge them and address them as relative equals) and more generally with institutions (schools and doctors, in particular). Through the example set by their parents, as well as through a range of daily practices and interactions, the children in these families "were trained in 'the rules of the game' that govern interactions with institutional representatives," were convinced of their "right to pursue their own individual preferences," and were "comfortable" in institutional settings, whether they were asking a teacher to "accommodate [their] individual learning style" or a doctor to deal with a skin reaction to a deodorant (Lareau 2011: 1–9).

In poor, working-class families, on the other hand, the study did not find the same parental practices of "concerted cultivation" but identified instead processes relating to the "accomplishment of natural growth." "Eliciting their children's feelings, opinions and thoughts" is not considered as important or done as frequently in these families, in which parents "see a clear boundary between adults and children." In terms of exercising authority, they "tend to use directives: they tell their children what to do rather than persuading them with reasoning." However, they exert far less control over leisure activities, which are less organized and tend to be managed by the children themselves who "are free to go out and play with friends and relatives who typically live close by." Within these families, "the cultural logic of child rearing at home is out of synch with the standards of institutions" and the parents' relationships with the latter tend to be more tense and even conflictual, which means that through everyday family socialization and interactions with schools and medical professionals, for example, they pass on to their children a "sense of distance, distrust and constraint in their institutional experiences" (Lareau 2011: 3). The children learn either to accept or secretly to resist institutional expectations rather than openly confronting them in a way considered legitimate in the middle classes. Moreover, the class culture incorporated by the children is sometimes in strong contradiction with school standards (for example, when they consider using physical violence to defend themselves to be normal) and this further accentuates the hiatus between family and school.

Lareau underlines that this opposition between concerted cultivation and natural growth should not be seen as suggesting that middle-class parents are more invested in, and work harder at, educating their children than their working-class counterparts. "The accomplishment of natural growth" also involves taking an engaged approach to parenting and working hard at child-rearing. Lareau shows, however, that in practical terms, working-class families define this endeavor differently from middle-class families. First, they do not organize their children's leisure time because they do not consider it to be their responsibility. Second, assertively intervening in their children's school experiences is difficult for them, owing to their own relationship to the institution and their levels of cultural capital, and it is also something for which they do not feel responsible. Therefore "the working class and poor parents" in Lareau's study "carried out their chores, drew boundaries and restrictions around their children, and then, within these limits, allowed their children to carry out their lives" (2011: 385, n. 2).

It is also important to note that these differences are not about how "severe" parents are. Based on some of these examples, it would be easy to jump to the conclusion that there is an opposition between working-class laxity and middle-class soft authoritarianism – and there is no shortage of social stereotypes to encourage such an assumption. However, the differentiated modes in which authority is exercised according to social class are far more complex than that and cannot be reduced to a simple contrast between authority and permissiveness – this is also true of the reverse hypothesis (based on the role of discipline by force in working-class educational approaches), which is no more accurate. In the education of the middle classes studied by Lareau, the importance of reminding children of the rules and explaining the reasons for actions ("talk, talk, talk") is clear. This educational mode therefore seems particularly likely to produce socialization effects of the order of self-constraint. In a sense, its very aim is to disappear as its requisites are progressively internalized. Analyzing working-class socialization practices shows that the same is not true in that context. While certain injunctions must be followed, they leave considerable freedom outside the rules they fix, for example where leisure activities are concerned. Moreover, working-class families tend to "keep things short and simple," and the use of directives produces an ad hoc education that does not count on the internalization of self-constraint. Children are expected to obey without discussion, that is to say without appropriating the action, which remains an adult directive. Finally, punishments are contextualized and immediate, also suggesting that the idea of authority exercised upon children outside the parents' physical presence, through internalized behavioral principles, is not very prevalent in working-class families. The difference here is therefore not so much a contrast between instilling "self-direction" in middle-class children and "conformity" in working-class children (Weininger et al. 2009), but rather, more fundamentally, the different role given to learning self-constraint in family class socialization.

Primary socialization is therefore very different depending on a family's position in the social space. Let us now look in more detail at some of the important areas in which these differences can be seen and on which sociologists have focused in particular.

2.2.4 *Play and social class*

One example is the case of childhood toys and play. Today, play is seen as both inherent to childhood and a universal aspect of children's behavior. However, types of play and toys, and how they are used, differ considerably according to a family's class position and therefore produce differentiated socialization effects.

Pioneering studies on play in the 1960s and 1970s by Basil Bernstein in Great Britain and Jean-Claude Chamboredon in France showed that the use of educational games and toys, viewed as learning opportunities, could better prepare children for the requirements of the education system (Bernstein and Young 1967; Chamboredon and Prévot 2015). Chamboredon's and Prévot's ground-breaking 1973 study demonstrated, for example, that upper- or middle-class families with high cultural capital are much more likely than working-class families to use "learning through play" as a means for instilling educational content in their children and to "bring school into the home" (2015: 168).[3] This use of play depends on economic factors, in terms not only of disposable income (to meet the cost of games and toys) but also of other considerations, such as space (the size of the home and whether or not the child has their own room affects the extent to which games are played). It also requires certain cultural conditions to be fulfilled, in particular parents perceiving the educational value of toys based on at least partial knowledge of child development theories – something Chamboredon and Prévot consider necessary for inspiring or guiding educational play. Finally, the authors also bring to bear on this issue socially differentiated representations of the division between work and leisure. In the working classes, working conditions – for example, difficult and/or dangerous work, considerable constraints due to supervision or surveillance – explain the fact that there is a strong opposition between the two. In this context, the very possibility of play being educational may well be set aside, with all responsibility for cultural transmission entrusted to the school system. In families with high levels of cultural capital, however, there is more likely to be greater continuity, in both practices and representations, between "play" and "work." The "pedagogy of play" therefore fits within a particular relationship to the world, which is that of the cultivated classes.

Studies of this kind show how different classes have different attitudes towards work and play, as well as to what constitute the "proper boundaries between them." Forty years after Chamboredon, and in a different national setting, Jessi Streib found this to be the case among her subjects decades after their primary socialization. The spouses from white-collar backgrounds were happy to wrap themselves up in their work and saw leisure time as an opportunity to expand their cultural horizons, outside the home, perhaps abroad, enjoying travel and adventurous, active holidays, while their blue-collar counterparts saw work as "just a job" and leisure as a "time to relax," at home watching television or engaging in activities in the local neighborhood (2015: 94–120). Approaching these questions in terms of class socialization shows how the differences in sensibilities that appear in adulthood have in fact been incorporated long before then, through daily, seemingly insignificant, repeated play with one type of toy or another.

2.2.5 Space and time

As we have already begun to see, analyzing class socialization requires paying particular attention to children's material conditions of existence, that is to say their tangible environment, the spaces and objects that surround them, their parents' economic situation, their family's living conditions, etc. We shall now look in more detail at some of the spatial but also temporal considerations relevant to class socialization.

Space and time might easily seem to be fixed physical attributes or contexts in which social variations can take place but that cannot themselves vary, any more than individuals' relationships to them can. However, on the contrary, space and time are at once socially structured (spaces and timeframes are social and vary according to a family's class position) and socially structuring (socialization can occur through the spaces in which people live or where they spend time, as well as through family habits and attitudes regarding time, which will lead to certain types of dispositions, categories of perception, tastes, or practical habits being incorporated).

In Durkheimian terms, space can be defined as a "physical environment" and a "configuration of things," made up of people and things brought together and arranged in a certain order, which can therefore be considered as a constraining frame, an "active factor" weighing upon the course of social phenomena and especially upon the shaping of the individuals that occupy and inhabit it (Cayouette-Remblière et al. 2019). As one study has shown, a "neighborhood" is the locus for very specific socialization processes, whether it is bourgeois, working-class, or suburban: growing up in a privately owned individual house in a new suburban housing development, "designed around a common street or little square," means growing up in a particular way, with tight intra-youth sociability and a shared stance towards "youth from the housing projects" (Cartier et al. 2016: 105–32).

Housing also constitutes a fairly obvious form of spatial variation from one social class to another – whether a home is spacious or not, how it is furnished, whether bedrooms and bathrooms are shared or not, and so on. The same is true for habits related to travel – whether one has ever left one's town or city, taken a plane, or has parents who possess second homes. The very definitions of the "space" to be considered are subject to social variations insofar as today some fractions of the dominant classes experience what could be called "international socialization" producing its own set of dispositions – for example, speaking a foreign language, having the ability and desire to engage in mobility and cosmopolitan living, both in the family and at work – that turn foreign countries into a familiar local space for certain families and their children (Wagner 2020).

Children therefore also experience "spatial socialization," which entails learning a particular relationship to housing and to space (a socialization *to* space that is about learning how to inhabit it) and an intrinsically spatial mode of learning various other things (a socialization *through* space, in which space leads to the incorporation of very diversified relationships to the social world, for example a feeling of exclusion or relegation in neighborhoods considered "bad" and a sense of ease and entitlement in bourgeois neighborhoods).

This duality (socialization through space and socialization to space) is clear in the early twentieth-century historical processes that Viviana Zelizer has retraced. After children became sacralized, "saving child life meant changing the daily activities of city children, pushing them indoors into playrooms or schoolrooms or designing special 'child' public spaces, such as playgrounds" (Zelizer 1985: 52). Parents and children alike were therefore socialized through space (new playgrounds, signs, etc.) to a certain relationship to risk and brought to think of the streets as being physically dangerous. This was not only a socialization to space, but also a socialization to a certain conception of childhood insofar as the streets became conceived as "socially inadequate" for children: "the proper place for a 'sacred' child was a protected environment, segregated from adult activities." These processes of spatial socialization affected working-class boys above all – this was very clear in the fact that they represented the group with the greatest reduction in child fatalities after these changes – insofar as girls' public activities were already limited, "and middle-class boys had already been partially domesticated" (52).

Furthermore, the temporal structure of family life intersects with these questions of space, and particular attitudes to time are also shaped and internalized during primary socialization. As Zerubavel notes "the replacement of the individual's internal biological clock by the conventional daily schedule of his or her social environment is a process which usually begins right at the very first days of infancy and is manifested by phenomena such as nursing babies by the clock rather than by demand. As Durkheim himself pointed out, it is definitely one of the most conspicuous accomplishments of primary socialization" (1981: 48). In some families, written tools such as calendars, diaries, schedules, and "to do" lists are used to objectivate, regulate, and structure time. This allows activities to be planned and enables a reflexive relationship to time management, congruent with the temporal requirements of the school environment, to be passed on to children (Lahire 2012b: 33–43). Once again, the different attitudes to time learned in childhood are rooted in class differences, especially regarding living conditions. In working-class environments, situations of economic precarity and atypical working hours can produce desynchronized family rhythms, irregular schedules, and periods of urgency that lead to fatalistic attitudes to both the present and the future. These attitudes, incorporated during primary family socialization, run counter to the temporal requirements that structure school activities (for example, the requirement to concentrate for a long time on a given task, or the temporal structure of reasoning and demonstration, e.g. "first, second," etc.) (Millet and Thin 2005). At the other end of the social spectrum, Lareau analyzed the temporal organization of day-to-day life in some of the upper-class families she studied. In these cases, the highly structured use of time, with frequent organized activities, resulted in the children incorporating a very different attitude to time, for example in the case of Alexander who complained that his mother "sign[ed him] up for everything" but who nevertheless acknowledged that his activities made him feel "special" and that without them his life would be "boring." He in fact felt disoriented when his schedule was not full, as illustrated by an excerpt from the investigator's field notes in which he was "grumpy" when he found out he had "nothing planned for the next day" (he did not count the fact he had school and "piano and guitar") (Lareau 2002: 754).

Finally, it is possible to look in even closer detail at variations in class socialization to time. In an ethnographic study focusing on students in France's highly selective *classes préparatoires* (post-secondary courses preparing students to sit the competitive entrance exams for the prestigious higher education institutions known as the Grandes Écoles) I showed that their attitudes towards time were linked to their social background and thus their family socialization (Darmon 2018). Inter-student variations could be explained, first, by the volume of capital they possessed. Some of them, from upper-class families, displayed considerable mastery of time. They defined themselves as being, generally speaking, "in sync" with both the general rhythm of the school year and their teachers' pace. They also developed techniques in order to remain so, defining time-management "principles" and adhering to them. Each week, they freed up time alongside their academic schedule for extra-curricular activities such as sport and music, and even when panicking about their heavy workload, they maintained these sessions. Some even enjoyed being under pressure, because they had incorporated a taste for it during their primary socialization – for example, one of them recalled always being "a bit hyperactive" and liking life to be "hectic," like his father, a CEO of a big company.

Conversely, for other students in the study, all from working-class families, time was something to which they were subjected rather than something they managed, something that was chronically lost, rather than something to be "taken." They constantly panicked about being behind in their work, but at the same time felt bored and as though time was passing too slowly. Their attitudes towards time are reminiscent of those present in their original background, deeply rooted both in economic insecurity and in working-class culture. These attitudes combine a feeling of precarious urgency, a sense of resignation about having no control over life's unexpected twists of fate, and a need to live in the present as a result of being unable to change the future.

However, the same study also suggests that types of capital, rather than just quantity, play a part in engendering specific attitudes towards time in children from middle- and upper-class families. Children from upper-class families who possess all kinds of capital (especially economic and cultural) have an "aristocratic" attitude to time (one must be lavish with one's time and with that of others, perhaps even wasting it in a form of conspicuous consumption aimed at "looking the part"), whereas children from upper-middle-class families with high cultural capital display a more bourgeois attitude to time (much more technical in nature, requiring, on the contrary, efficiently organizing and managing time in order to "save" it). This research therefore reveals "time-styles" that, like Bourdieu's "life-styles," seem to be connected to the forms of capital possessed by students (economic versus cultural) and not simply to the quantities of capital in question. It also highlights the differentiated forms of temporal socialization (including within the upper classes) that produce them (Darmon 2018). Relationships to time are learned at a very early stage during family or school socialization and it can be argued that they "constitute a relatively fundamental and profound element of relations to the world" that becomes "the basis for other processes of interiorization" (Darmon et al. 2019: 6).

Space and time are therefore not so much *a priori* physical facts as they are matrixes that result from complex processes of socialization and obey social laws and variations. Material living conditions therefore produce a relationship to economic constraints and space that profoundly differentiates working-class and bourgeois socialization. Richard Hoggart, writing an autobiography of his childhood and a sociology of the British working classes in which he grew up, retraced the specific material and cultural conditions of his primary socialization. He pieced together a daily life marked by the experience of poverty and the need to count everything so as to "manage" (Hoggart 1989: 43–6). While what bourgeois standards no doubt viewed as a "cluttered and congested" home could be experienced as a warm, gregarious "family centre" (Hoggart 1971: 33–4), these different conditions of socialization nevertheless produce a specific relationship to space and also involve internalizing one's place in society.

However, the experience of poverty in working-class environments does not mean that children are any less "spoilt," contrary to what summary judgments might assume. Economic constraints are not the only factor that determines how class socialization takes place. Class culture, whether bourgeois or working-class, also plays a role. Hoggart has shown how strong economic constraints in the working classes go hand-in-hand with a view of childhood as a period when one is protected from that constraint and in which children are all the more indulged because "there is all the rest of life to come," "yer only young once," and children should "'ave a good time while they can" (1971: 47). It is in light of this aspect of working-class culture that Hoggart interprets the care given to infants and children, the purchasing of expensive presents for them relative to the family's budget, and the way they are fed. The higher numbers of overweight and obese children among the working classes, noted earlier, may well be the "dark side" to these practices, just as anorexia is the "dark side" of middle- and upper-class practices of control and nutritional asceticism (Darmon 2017: 189–227). This aspect of working-class socialization identified by Hoggart in the 1950s has far from disappeared since and can still today serve to explain expensive presents (e.g. games consoles) and greater permissiveness about television and internet usage or bedtime, not as a reflection of irresponsible laxity but rather as a socially produced disposition to "enjoy the good times" while they last.

2.2.6 The class-based incorporation of Black masculinities

A third focal area – and another example of the huge gap between forms of class socialization at each end of the social spectrum – can be provided by looking at two studies on the making of Black masculinity.

Laurence Otis Graham's study, *Our Kind of People*, published in 1999, retraces the childhoods of the Black upper class who grew up in the very selective "Jack and Jill of America" organization, founded in 1938, that is "focused on bringing together children age 2 to 19" and in which "elite Black kids are separated from the rest." The organization's chapters serve as "a network for parents who want play groups for their children, as well as a network for young adults who want companionship, dating relationships, and ultimately marriage partners." For the children, this means living in all-white neighborhoods, "attend[ing] classes that ha[ve] never seen a Black face beyond the custodian's closet," and hearing their mothers planning a career for them as a banker, a doctor, a "litigator or some kind of judge," and expecting "more than advertising or entertainment" from someone who comes from a family of "professionals for two generations." It also means having the specific Black upper-class experience of attending "the right cotillions, summer camps and private schools." All these experiences turn children into a certain kind of people ("our kind of people"), like the fourteen-year-old boy described attending a Jack and Jill career day, with his "green cotton turtleneck" among a group of children whose "sophistication and elitism mixed so adroitly" that, the author writes, it was "like listening to conversations between me and my friends at age thirty-five" (Graham 1999: 36).

In stark contrast to this socialization, Ann Arnett Ferguson identifies very different processes in a study published the year after Graham's that focuses on twenty fifth- and sixth-grade African American boys from Rosa Parks Elementary School in a middle-sized city on the West Coast: ten "schoolboys," who were identified by the school as doing well, and ten "trouble-makers," identified as "getting into trouble." Ferguson's study links together the children's behavior at school with the "popular knowledge generated in family and neighborhood," that is to say, from the perspective of the present book, with the categories of perception and family practices that structure and organize these children's family socialization and account for the dispositions they incorporate. The study uncovers ways of seeing the world and dispositions that are shared among families and neighborhoods, that are incorporated through contact with them, and that directly affect how the boys deal with school. This includes, in particular, observation and experience as a method of obtaining knowledge and a critical and oppositional stance to authority. What appears is a very particular making of Black masculinity: "The theories, the stance, the style of communication that the boys bring to school are strategies, tools, that are forged in the contexts of family and public. All the families prepare their sons to inhabit a world in which they are in danger – an 'endangered species' – and inculcate them with forms of defense and survival" (Ferguson 2000: 133). Incorporating this sense of danger, in a context of social terror that arises out of a group condition, can be viewed as the polar opposite of the way in which the upper-class boys in Graham's study incorporate social ease (especially in their relationship to school and institutions more broadly). Furthermore, although in both cases family socialization can lead to the boys challenging authority, it is clear how this differs in each case, on the one hand taking an accepted form for the institution and reflecting ease and confidence, and on the other taking an unaccepted form and relating to survival reflexes.

Moreover, Ferguson's study shows more fine-grained, internal variations in family class socialization and its products than simply an opposition between the upper and the working classes. Within the working and lower-middle classes on which her study focuses, she distinguishes two types of family socialization according to the families' social position (in other words, according to different class "fractions"). Of course, all the parents of the young Black males she studied are "filled with dread" about what might happen to their sons in the "bad neighborhood" they live in. They "especially worry that the boys will do something that will entangle them in 'the system'" (i.e. the criminal justice system) (Ferguson 2000: 107) and as a result they develop "survival strategies" that they pass on to their children. This transmission can occur explicitly through lessons and education (one father, for example, recounts how he always insists that his son carries money so as to be viewed as a "respectable" consumer in a shop), or it can take place by tacit example in everyday situations witnessed by the children (for example, potentially humiliating administrative situations such as rent-board hearings). These "strategies" – in Bourdieu's sense of the word, that is to say a sometimes unconscious strategy, a socially determined way of envisaging and solving a problem (1977: 36) – are of two very distinct orders, however. The first strategy can be seen in families belonging to the lower fractions of the middle classes and is part of a worldview in which parents anticipate "upward mobility for their sons through school achievement." They "prescribe strategies of 'racelessness' in the presentation of self" (i.e. clothes, demeanor, etc.) and "avoidance to deal with racism," along with efforts to control anger, avoid confrontation, and not "fight back." "The second strategy is found in poor families who feel unable to protect their kids from the exigencies of the real world. Their kids must learn how to stand up for themselves and play more adult roles." They learn to deal with the world – to be "fighters, both verbally and physically" or to "challenge people who have power" over them – through direct observation and emulation, as well as explicitly from their families. The troublemakers are more often from these families and expect to be "engaged in confrontations with authority, to be able to stand up for themselves, to talk back, to defend themselves physically" (Ferguson 2000: 133).

Variations in the family class socialization of "schoolboys" and "troublemakers" therefore produce individual differences between them, just as the variations between the socialization in these working-class/lower-middle-class families and the upper-class families mentioned earlier produces more visible and striking differences. In these cases, class socialization has therefore created real, systematic differences between Black teenagers of the same age and sex, which are far more subtle than a simple contrast between "rebellious" working classes and "obedient" upper classes, or between subjugated lower classes and entitled higher classes. It is also clear that approaching these issues via socialization not only makes it possible to examine these variations in detail, it also – and in fact above all, since this is the principal aim – sheds light on how these differences come to be, how they are constructed, learned, and incorporated through processes of socialization.

These comparisons between the extreme features of class positions that are polar opposites (the very highest fractions of the bourgeoisie and the very poorest among the working classes) inevitably result in some measure of caricature. However, they also identify the two "ends" of the spectrum between which the range of differences in class socialization lie. The immense gap separating these examples is not an empty space; it is composed of a multitude of variations that make up the social space of the social classes.

Many examples can serve to illustrate these variations, particularly since, following Bourdieu and as we have already seen, it can be argued that differences result not only from how *much* capital people have, but also from what *kinds* of capital they have. Socialization will be different in upper-middle-class families defined by high levels of economic capital, such as families of business owners without graduate qualifications, and those whose "wealth" and social position is primarily defined by their cultural capital, for example academics; it will also be different among tradesmen and among low-level municipal employees who hold a graduate qualification. This therefore opens up even more questions that can be investigated through the prism of class socialization and the broad range of variations it brings to light.

Finally, before concluding this overview of class socialization, it is important to recall that these differences are also inequalities, insofar as the forms of socialization that take place in middle- and upper-class families enjoy greater recognition, are considered more legitimate, and are more in sync with the requisites of the school institution or the world of work, but also, as Lareau reminds us, with those of administrative or medical settings. Following Bourdieu, it can be argued that school is the archetypal example illustrating how the "profitability" of family socialization can differ, with some children being, as Calarco (2018) puts it, "coached for the classroom." However, even social inequalities in health (that produce very considerable differences in life expectancy according to social background and socio-economic status) are partly rooted in relationships to medical institutions and the way in which, at a very young age, children learn how to behave in front of a doctor, but also how to experience symptoms and pain, or not, and how to express them, or not (Boltanski 1971). People are socialized to health (to somatic sensations and pain, to a given relationship to the medical world, etc.) and healthy or unhealthy bodies are produced from a very early age. These areas remain largely understudied by the sociology of socialization, but explain the persisting, clear socio-economic gradient in health in developed countries (Singh-Manoux and Marmot 2005). The different forms of class socialization mentioned here therefore have effects in areas as fundamental as schooling, employment, health, and life expectancy.

2.3 Gender socialization

While historical periods and social class "fashion" children differently, they do not always fashion the same children within the same period or the same social class: for example, is the socialization of Black working-class girls the same as that of Black working-class boys? Are brothers and sisters born into the same family at the same time period not raised differently?

2.3.1 Incorporating gender

The last major "fold" of socialization that we shall look at here is that of the difference between genders. Primary and family socialization play a huge role in the process of differentiation between individuals who are considered to be "male" or "female," especially because this is when models of gendered behavior are most "silently" internalized and are most likely to be imposed as self-evident and natural.

As early as the 1950s, functionalist approaches such as that adopted by Parsons provided tools for thinking about gender socialization (through the internalization of roles determined by sex). These approaches were, however, strongly marked on the one hand by psychoanalysis and, on the other, by a normative conception of what these "sex roles" were: "the father role is, *relative to the others* high both on power and on 'instrumentality' – hence low on 'expressiveness'. The mother role is high on power and on 'expressiveness', thus low in instrumentality. The son role is low on power but high on instrumentality, the daughter low on power but high on expressiveness – hence low on instrumentality" (Parsons and Bales 1955: 45). From this perspective, sex-role identification ensures both the individual's integration within the social system and his or her early adaptation to the gendered division of social roles, defined *ex ante* as strictly differentiating between the masculine role of instrumental leader, providing income, protection, and discipline, and the feminine role of expressive leader, providing love, care, and emotional support, learned respectively by little boys and little girls.

The notion of gender socialization, however, allows us to understand and analyze how society constructs the children who are seen as little boys differently from those who are seen as little girls, whilst avoiding psychoanalytical or normative views, and displacing the perspective from that of the internalization of social roles to the incorporation of gendered habitus or dispositions, which can be entirely unconscious. As we shall see, unlike functionalist approaches, this type of approach offers the possibility of accounting for atypical cases of gender socialization.

This shift in perspective leads us, as described earlier, to see socialization as *incorporation* and to look closely at how society builds men's and women's bodies differently. The incorporation of the habitus that are produced by gender socialization offers a particularly salient example of the strength and realities of incorporation, which mean that "the essential part of the learning of masculinity and femininity tends to inscribe the difference between the sexes in bodies (especially through clothing), in the form of ways of walking, talking, standing, looking, sitting, etc." (Bourdieu 2000: 141). If we focus, for example, on ways of walking, we can return again to Marcel Mauss's classic text on techniques of the body, in which he describes how young Maori girls learn a gait that involves swinging their hips by imitating their mothers and following their explicit instructions. Innumerable examples, whether older or more contemporary, testify to the way in which models to imitate, explicit corporeal education, or factors such as clothing, shoes, hairstyles, and activities, implicitly or explicitly, gently or violently, "constrain" boys' and girls' bodies to adopt different ways of walking.

This is evident in all the work done to inscribe gender difference into children's bodies from a very early age: blue and pink, trousers and skirts, hairstyles, earrings, and so on. From early childhood, differentiated clothing and accessories instill particular relationships to the body: one does not walk, stand, or sit the same way in trousers and in a skirt, and socially one is not permitted to engage in the same attitudes and activities, which therefore instills different habits in terms of the relationship to space (and the social world). These processes could be considered outdated in a world that is much more gender fluid than the one described by Parsons and Bales in the 1950s, but when it comes to gender socialization it is important not to be too hasty in assuming that it is a product of bygone days and that there has since been a radical change. We know that even today, little boys and little girls tend not to be dressed in the same way (even when the latter wear trousers) or given the same toys, and that toy-store Christmas catalogues and websites still offer a veritable Madame Tussauds' display of gender differences.

Many studies offer insight into how socialization genders bodies (i.e. how it produces differently gendered bodies) and how gender habitus (ways of seeing the world, tastes, sensibilities, the propensity to act in this way or that, or to think this or that) are incorporated during the socialization process. Since the 1970s, research has shown the "influence of social conditioning on the formation of the feminine role in young childhood" (Gianini Belotti 1999) and has allowed us both to "understand how the 'masculine' comes (or does not come) to men and boys" and to "examine how gendered ways of thinking and doing, located on the side of the 'male' sex, are internalized" (Bertrand et al. 2015).

Gender socialization begins even before birth, with the future baby's room and clothes. Even when parents deliberately and openly choose to distance themselves from stereotypes associating particular clothes or colors with each sex (pink for girls, blue for boys), there is still strong incorporation of these tropes – for example, choosing "neutral" colors, rather than flipping the traditional binary, or abandoning neutral clothing in the infant's first months (Samuel et al. 2014).

Finally, even though babies' bodies are so similar at birth, they can still give rise to very gendered perceptions and categorizations, contrasting "big" boys with girls who are "more likely to be described as beautiful, pretty, and cute, and as resembling their mothers," as one study has shown (Rubin et al. 1974: 512). In this respect, the same study concluded that fathers seem to produce more extreme and stereotyped rating judgments of their newborns than mothers. Similarly, perception of the same baby's emotional state can vary according to the sex it has been ascribed. In another study, when confronted with the same emotional response displayed by an infant, subjects labeled it "anger" if the infant was thought to be a boy, and "fear" if the infant was thought to be a girl (Condry and Condry 1976). All this therefore shows that "sex-typing and sex-role socialization appear to have already begun their course at the time of the infant's birth, when information about the infant is minimal" (Rubin et al. 1974: 519).

Despite the relative lack of differentiation between babies' bodies during their first months, gender socialization is therefore already at work in various ways. In a classic Italian study on gender "conditioning," Elena Gianini Belotti points to the multiple social channels through which sex differentiation takes place. Babies are fed differently according to whether they are boys or girls. A big appetite is considered normal among the boys, and even encouraged, whereas baby girls are required to have a more moderate appetite and are trained to be delicate. Parents intervene in different ways when boys and girls do the same things (screaming, laughing or speaking too loudly, forgetting to be polite, and not showing affection for other children is far less accepted among girls but, conversely, they are allowed to cry or show fear much more than boys). Parents even teach their children differently, for example showing a girl how to throw a ball and a boy how to kick it. In short, adults automatically select how to act with their children according to their children's biological sex (Gianini Belotti 1999: 76–7)

2.3.2 Games, leisure, and sports
The early childhood years reinforce differentiation between children and perceptions of these differences. Gender socialization continues, drawing on the vast range of childhood "objects" and material conditions (clothes, books or magazines, leisure activities, toys) that makes up all the instances of this gender socialization.

For example, toys and games are just as divisive in terms of gender as they are in terms of social class. Traditionally, girls tend to have more dolls and domestic items (toys that reproduce their assignation to the domestic sphere, care, and motherhood) whereas boys have more mechanical tools, sports equipment, and large and small vehicles in their rooms (toys that foster mobility, a relationship to the outside world, and physical strength). Once again, it may seem as though things are changing, particularly when parents try to avoid what they consider gender stereotypes, but studies still reveal certain constants – for example when parents in theory refuse to categorize toys as being for boys or girls, but in practice reproduce gender assignations, or when fathers display more rigid stereotyped expectations relative to mothers. The sociology of gender has also shown that girls enjoy greater flexibility in terms of the toys with which they play (Wood et al. 2002) and that masculinity is much better tolerated in girls than femininity in boys (Kane 2006).

In terms of "family" childhood activities, a study observing middle-class families has shown that a simple visit to the zoo can involve gender socialization and processes naturalizing social differences. First, the adults in the study attributed gender to zoo animals by projecting onto them human characteristics associated with feminine and masculine stereotypes – the gorilla had big hands "like Daddy," or the large male gorilla was the Dad and the smaller male gorilla was the Mom. Second, the mothers and fathers perceived, reacted to, and drew their children's attention to the animals differently, particularly according to their own gender dispositions (with the mothers giving more emphasis to the zoo animals' esthetic features and fathers emphasizing instead their strength, dexterity, and dangerousness). Finally, the adults disciplined boys and girls differently in the context of the zoo's built environment, for example underscoring their daughters' risk of bodily harm, disciplining them more than their sons, and placing greater constraints on their physical activity and adventurousness, while allowing their sons to be much more physically expressive. In doing so, these adults served as agents of socialization to conventional gendered behavior. The visit to the zoo was therefore a moment when gender norms and expected behaviors were transmitted, but also when the gender stereotypes "associated with the biological determinism of the natural living world" were legitimated and naturalized (Garner and Grazian 2016).

Later, and right through to adolescence, the use of free time (i.e. outside school) whether devoted to leisure or work, is also significant and produces differentiated socialization effects according to gender. Different practices can be observed between boys and girls in terms of the musical instruments or video games they play and how they use the internet. Their socialization to space is also deeply gendered. Studies have shown that while girls tend initially to be considered more mature and autonomous than boys, and are allowed to move around freely during the day at an earlier age, there is a gradual inversion of the degree of autonomy granted as they grow older. Girls learn to inhabit the urban space differently than boys, and from a more restrictive and dominated perspective. The urban socialization of girls is therefore "doubly differentiated." First, they experience specific interactions in public spaces, such as wolf-whistles, compliments, or being followed, which they are taught to consider as normal or at least as potentially recurrent. There is also the perception of the street as an arena for encounters that are threatening or, at the very least, uncomfortable. Second, they receive special attention from their parents, who supervise their urban practices and tend to be stricter with them than with boys about acceptable clothing and going out at night (Rivière 2012). We have already seen this sort of socialization to and through space with class socialization. Where learning gender through space is concerned, it is worth recalling Erving Goffman's classic text in which he reminds us that "toilet segregation" (the fact that women and men's toilets are often very visibly separated) is in no way justified by biological functions or organs: this arrangement "is presented as a natural consequence of the difference between the sex-classes, when in fact it is rather a mean of honoring, *if not producing*, the difference" (Goffman 1977: 316).

There are also gender differences in the sports played in childhood and adolescence. For boys, sport is often a locus for the reproduction of masculinity and especially the "tendency to utilize violence against others to achieve a goal," as Michael Messner has shown. For example, violence is virtually non-existent among young boys just starting to play hockey and "few males truly enjoy hitting and being hit," but they nonetheless progressively learn "rough play" (1992: 66–7) as a strategy but also as a reflex, or even something for which they develop a taste that testifies to the incorporation of gendered dispositions.

In this area too, when changes take place, it is always in the same direction, with girls engaging in "boys' sports" such as soccer without boys starting to do rhythmic gymnastics. Even when a practice does change and takes into account shifts in gendered representations, for example cheerleading in which strength and technique are now valued, it nevertheless continues to reproduce, legitimate, and teach the esthetic norms that weigh upon girls: the importance of the ideal female body, of the esthetics of movement and appearance, of the suppleness and constant smile required. "Cheerleaders, for all their athleticism, toughness, and risk taking, do not disrupt twenty-first century, taken-for-granted notions of normative femininity and masculinity" and "ultimately do not challenge the status quo by transgressing gendered boundaries" (Adams and Bettis 2003: 88).

For the sociology of socialization, however, the issue at stake is not just shedding light on adults' gendered attitudes towards, or practices with, children, nor bringing out differences between boys and girls that can theoretically be "ascribed" to socialization. Rather, this approach aims to analyze in detail in which circumstances, through which *processes* and *practices*, and as a result of which discourses, the agents of socialization present in the child's environment lead that child to develop dispositions that either are or are not characteristic of their gender class.

Parsons' classic framework of the internalization of sex roles posited that socialization leads to pre-established roles – instrumental, for boys, expressive for girls – being integrated and that socialization has failed when these roles are not "well" integrated. This is where the gender socialization approach differs insofar as it can also account for so-called "atypical" childhood socialization by considering, for example, the social logics that result in someone becoming an appearance-conscious little girl or a tomboy, an appearance-conscious boy or an athletic one, a girl who is a footballer or a boy who is a ballet dancer, and later in life a man who is a midwife or a woman who is a lorry driver. A study of the transmission of family dispositions among the small minority of middle-class boys "who don't like sports" analyzed the "socialization modes involved in the construction of an atypical gender *habitus*": a lack of interest in competitive sports, distance from physically aggressive behavior, and a taste for artistic activities, for example, were incorporated within families belonging to the category of "humanistic intellectuals" with a "cultivated lifestyle," but also within specific family configurations such as all-male sibships, "as though the absence of girls somehow limits the extent of father-to-son transmission while promoting mother-to-son proximity" (Mennesson et al. 2019). Gender socialization can therefore not only explain how the taste for sports comes to most boys but also how others come to stand apart from that majority and not like sports. With these atypical cases, the influence of family gender socialization is therefore even more apparent because it counters alleged biological or sociological "nature" and takes precedence.

Gender socialization therefore creates differences between individuals. There is more though: just like class socialization, it also creates inequalities in the same process. The consequences of gender socialization affect women unequally in the academic sphere (particularly in terms of educational career choices), the professional and public spheres (salaries, professional responsibilities, positions in elected office), and the private sphere (sexuality, the domestic economy). We shall see a little later in this book how the different regimes of inequality (class, gender, but also race) link together, not from the point of view of their general intersectionality but more precisely in terms of a sociology of socialization seeking to understand how we become what we are and what makes us act or think one way rather than another.

In conclusion: we have so far been able to take the measure of (1) the strength of primary socialization and the importance of childhood as a moment when dispositions are built; (2) the difference between education (a child-rearing program, with explicit principles and values) and socialization (an incorporated process and its, sometimes largely unconscious, results within the individual), and (3) the importance of practice within a theory of socialization based on material conditions of existence.

Until now, in keeping with the sociological theories underpinning this chapter, I have looked at all these issues whilst focusing on one of the main agents of primary socialization, namely the family. However, other agents have emerged in the background of the analyses and examples discussed – specific family members rather than "the family" in general, school, space, books, childhood objects, peers, and so on. The next chapter will take these elements and place them in the foreground, focusing on the plural nature of primary socialization that has, so far, been understated.

2
Building People II: The Plurality of Primary Socialization

After having read the last chapter, it might seem evident that primary socialization can be equated with family socialization. Are parents not socially and legally responsible for raising their children? Are individuals not first and foremost shaped by their families? And is it not through the family, and the family alone, that society first exerts its influence? Having said that, it is difficult to imagine a world in which children only come into contact with their parents, even in the early years. It is therefore necessary to continue exploring primary socialization by considering how far it can extend beyond the family unit itself.

It would not, however, be enough for such an analysis simply to list the people and institutions that children "come into contact with," as I have just perhaps too lightly suggested. We have to ask whether these contacts actually have a socializing effect, since they could very easily take place without any particular consequences for the individual's construction. Keeping this question in mind, let us now examine primary socialization further by focusing on its multiplicity, building out from the premise that not everything that is played out in childhood is played out in the family …

It would be tempting, in doing so, to retrace the history of how agents of primary socialization have varied over time. However, falling back on the idea of an unequivocal "march of history" that has led to the current situation – instead of trying to produce a socio-history of socialization processes, which is still needed – is not necessarily the most productive approach. The different hypotheses put forward about the "family monopoly" on primary socialization illustrate this well. Two competing points of view arguing, respectively, that the family has acquired or has lost this monopoly would appear, on the face of it, to be equally convincing. The argument that the family has progressively acquired the monopoly on primary socialization is present in Norbert Elias's work, for example. According to him, ever since the Middle Ages, the "task of early conditioning" has gradually fallen "more and more exclusively to parents" (1994: 158, 153), whereas previously it fell to the higher echelons of society (conditioning those below them), to peers, or to all those in the child's immediate environment, whether family or servants. Elias argues that, from the nineteenth century onwards, this task then became the parents' sole responsibility (1994: 116–17, 119, 158–9). The opposing argument, according to which the family has lost this monopoly, argues instead that the current situation (i.e. plural primary socialization) testifies to a process that also dates back at least to the nineteenth century, in which social changes – for example, evolving educational norms, children's schooling, and, more recently, women's increased participation in the workforce and its impact on modes of childcare – explain the family's waning monopoly on childhood socialization.

It is possible that these two processes simply came one after another, with the slow acquisition of a monopoly until the nineteenth century followed by a more rapid decline during the twentieth. However, it is perhaps instead the very notion of family monopoly, in any epoch, that should be called into question. Many agents of primary socialization began competing with the family's influence long before the second half of the twentieth century. These include states and churches across the Western world, but also, in the upper classes, servants and nursemaids, governesses and private tutors, boarding schools and other educational institutions, or monasteries and convents; in the working classes they have included apprenticeships and early entry into the world of work, as well as educational or reform institutions (orphanages, asylums, reform schools, and so on) designed to take in and control poor children, and, in the United States, plantations, where enslaved African American children were generally separated from their parents (Grant 2013; Schmidt 2013; Gutman 2013). It is therefore difficult to frame the nineteenth century as the century of a family monopoly that has since been lost.

This does not mean, however, that the twentieth and twenty-first centuries have been characterized by a family monopoly that has replaced prior plural influences. The aim of this chapter is precisely to refute that hypothesis. To do so, I begin by defining the diverse influences that operate during primary socialization, including within the family itself, and by taking the measure of their impact. When attention is paid to internal diversity and variations, it is possible to identify and examine the groups, institutions, or extra-familial individuals also involved in processes of primary socialization. This chapter begins by focusing on the people tasked with "looking after" children; it then looks at the experts or professionals who affect their education either directly or via educational norms; and finally it considers their peers in the school environment. It is important to note that the strength of primary socialization is not diluted across these multiple agents; quite the contrary, this approach reveals the full measure of the impact that primary socialization can have because together the different agents in question make up the diverse channels through which society turns us into the people we become.

1. Plural influences

In research, there is often a risk of only finding what we are looking for. If, in order to address the question of primary socialization, we only focus on the family circle – an approach that also involves certain normative assumptions about what primary socialization is "supposed" to be – there is a strong chance that it will seem as though the family influence operates to the exclusion of all others. It is therefore necessary to extend the investigative field further and to look specifically at what happens elsewhere, but also to look differently at what happens in the family. From this perspective, the theory of socialization elaborated by Bernard Lahire (2002; 2004; 2011; 2012b; 2013) is an invaluable tool because it advocates systematically tracing all the possible plurality and variation at work.

1.1 From plural socialization to the "plural actor"

The contribution of this theory should first be linked to its methodological and epistemological stance. On the one hand, this means considering socialization as an empirical question to be framed and answered by analyzing materials that have been collated through fieldwork; on the other hand, it means not hesitating to look to the micro-sociological level of the individual in order to identify the effect of social structures. It is even possible to adjust the focus of our "sociological microscope" so that it points to the infra-individual and allows us to observe specific dispositions (ways of doing, seeing, or feeling things, inclinations to act or believe, and so on) that have been internalized during the socialization process. This approach differs from the perspectives usually adopted to analyze the sociogenesis of habitus insofar as it looks at each area of practice in which dispositions are incorporated, rather than immediately considering the system they form or the overall principle producing them.

Socialization often seems to be a sort of impenetrable black box, but thanks to this type of "genetic and dispositionalist sociology of socialization" (Lahire 2005: 305), focused on the genesis of individual dispositions, it is possible to open up that box and break it down into situated agents, modes, and effects. Far from only considering the *results* of socialization – envisioned as a magical or presupposed mechanism – the task facing sociology is to study in detail *processes* of socialization in childhood and adolescence, from two main perspectives. First, examining different forms of socialization – whether in the family, at school, in the peer group, or in cultural, sporting, political, or religious institutions – and the processes through which dispositions and values are incorporated. Second, examining how mental and behavioral dispositions can be transferred from one sphere to another (e.g. from the family to school, from school to the family) and considering the tension between contradictory dispositions in the case of socializing frameworks that are partly, or totally, incompatible (Lahire 2005: 305–7). For if the family is not the only agent of primary socialization, then there is nothing to guarantee that the heterogeneous and potentially contradictory socializing principles of the various agents involved will converge (Lahire 2011: 22).

Viewed from this perspective, dispositions are therefore "situated" with respect to the context in which they were internalized, that is to say in terms both of the area of practice concerned (school dispositions, sporting dispositions, etc.) and of the agents through which they were acquired (school, sports club, etc.). These situated products may be transferable to other areas of practice or not (a serious school disposition may or may not find the necessary conditions to be actualized on the football field, while an ascetic sporting disposition may or may not be actualized in the classroom). Differences in behavior from one context to another are not the product of a single habitus (resulting from a single process of socialization) that is "refracted" in different contexts; rather, they are the product of different dispositions relative to given contexts and areas of practice, and acquired through distinct processes of socialization. Each individual therefore carries plural dispositions, which will be activated or put on standby according to the context (Lahire 1999: 136–7). In order to understand "why individuals or groups do what they do, think what they think, feel what they feel," it is therefore necessary to consider their practices in light of both their social properties and the contexts in which their actions unfold, and to combine "dispositionalism" with "contextualism," as evidenced by Lahire's equation "dispositions + context = practices," which could be expanded into incorporated past + present context = observable practices" (Lahire 2012a: 21–7).

Because the influence of society can be found in people's "most intimate folds," including during sleep when they seem most entirely disconnected from ordinary social realities, this framework can even be used to understand dreams – or more precisely why we dream about the things we dream about (rather than about other things) and in one particular form (rather than another) – and to locate the reasons in the dreamer's incorporated past. Lahire suggests interpreting dreams by connecting the dream to the dreamer's dispositions (some of which may have begun to be formed in early childhood), to their "existential situation" in the period in which they are dreaming (the problems they are facing, their concerns or obsessions), to contextual factors in the immediate past that have sparked off the dream (for example, the day before), and to the sleep context in which the animated images of the dream take shape. In dreams as in the rest of social life, the past is not an inert stock of memories, it is an active structure, a principle of action, and a powerful driving force that helps define what is meaningful and important and what is not (Lahire 2020).

From this perspective, it is therefore because socialization is "plural" that it fashions what Lahire terms "plural actors." Heterogeneous socialization processes and products are the rule, and homogeneity is the exception. The coherency of habitus – in which, as a result of converging socialization processes, a single generating principle directs behavior in different areas of practice – is a particular case that requires particular conditions of internalization. For example, while high-level athletes' long, systematic, intense socialization is likely to result in a sporting habitus, simply playing a sport (even regularly) is more likely only to produce specific dispositions that may well not be activated outside the sports field (Lahire 2005: 318).

1.2 The social conditions of socialization

Lahire's call to take into account variations in socialization processes can be briefly summarized in the following "law": "every (individual) body plunged into a plurality of social worlds is subjected to heterogeneous and sometimes contradictory principles of socialization that they embody" (Lahire 2011: 26).

It is important, however, to avoid interpreting this "law" in too mechanical a fashion. Simply being "plunged" into a social world (or "in contact" with it, as I said at the very beginning of the chapter) is not sufficient for that world, and the individuals who inhabit it, to have real socialization effects. In this regard, Lahire's works can help us to identify some of the social conditions that make the socializing influence of given agents, contexts, or interactions effective.

Rather than considering that cultural capital is automatically passed on within the family when the family possesses that capital and the child is in contact with it, it is necessary to consider the concrete modes through which this transmission occurs and particularly "moments of, and opportunities for, socialization." Questions that might at first glance seem banal in fact prove essential: "which person holds the cultural capital?" "Does the person spend a lot of time with the child? Do they oversee the child's schooling?" The conditions for transmission of cultural capital can be difficult to achieve, for example if it is mainly possessed by a father who, owing to the gendered division of parenting roles or to professional constraints, is only moderately involved in his children's education. Similarly, it is harder if cultural heritage is present in the child's environment, but in a "dead, non-appropriated, and inappropriate" form, for example the encyclopedias and dictionaries that Lahire noted on one particular family's bookshelves but that, significantly, had their edges rather than their spines visible. Family "background" does not function in an abstract manner and it does not suffice for a child to be surrounded by cultural objects or by people with particular dispositions in order to internalize a certain relationship to culture: "presence" does not necessarily equate to "socializing effect" (Lahire 2012b: 217–25, 274–5).

To these practical conditions of possibility for socialization, it is important to add a more symbolic dimension in order to understand why not all contact, even prolonged, automatically results in socializing effects. This dimension can be labeled the *legitimacy* to socialize. Lahire proposes this hypothesis based on Maurice Halbwachs's analysis of how all the pomp and circumstance surrounding the judicial corps creates and reinforces a barrier between its members and the criminals they deal with on a daily basis. The aim is to prevent any "contagion" between the two groups, that is to say any socialization of the judges by the criminals. This suggests that socializing effects depend upon the legitimacy of being fashioned by a given agent and that both institutions and the hierarchies established by power relations are involved in determining this legitimacy. This could explain, for example, why the frequent contacts between servants and aristocrats' children or, in another context, between little girls and little boys, generally do not result in the former having socializing effects upon the latter. The idea of plural influences should therefore not be conflated with the idea of automatic socialization through contact alone. In each case, it is necessary to examine the social conditions that enable agents of socialization to have an impact – or not.

2. Intra-familial heterogeneity

Before beginning to take into account socializing influences beyond the family, it is necessary first to consider the extent to which intra-familial influences themselves can vary. In the previous chapter, I approached the "family" as though it were a single unit. However, "family" cannot be reduced to parents alone. Members of the extended family or siblings can also be considered agents of socialization, as Goffman suggests when he says that, in terms of gender socialization, the "household is a socializing depot" and that in mixed-gender sibships "each sex becomes a training device for the other, a device that is brought right into the house" (1977: 314).

From the point of view of socialization, the parental couple itself does not form a unified entity. Parents can, for example, come from different social backgrounds and therefore not have the same dispositions or share the same norms. In fact, the first difference between opposite-sex parents is gender: even if the parents have been constructed by similar experiences and come from similar backgrounds, they will, to use Berger and Luckmann's vocabulary, necessarily transmit feminine or masculine "versions" of reality to their children and it is impossible to calculate the sum total of these and define one "parental" transmission. The considerable gender difference between opposite-sex parents is also far from being the only intra-familial variation that needs to be taken into account. In his book *Tableaux de familles* (Family Portraits), Lahire examined the "family configurations" in which young third-graders were raised and sought to identify "secondary" differences in socialization between working-class families with similar incomes and low levels of education, particularly in terms of the effects upon school success or failure. In "statistical" terms, that is to say if we determine social status by the head of the family's occupation and qualifications (or lack thereof), these families were equivalent. However, Lahire's analysis revealed differences in socialization within working-class backgrounds that could explain the often substantial discrepancies between different children's performances at school. Thanks to micro-sociological analysis, the families' seeming equivalence was erased and, instead, the specific relationships that actually had socializing effects for the child were examined. For example, in families with parents in similar situations, the presence of a sister studying at university and tasked with monitoring her little brother's homework altered his socialization to school and culture. Similarly, a grandfather with school capital who regularly saw his grandchildren and passed on to them something of his attitude to the world was not equivalent to a grandfather with the same level of school capital but who was now deceased or who never saw his grandchildren. When examined in detail, statistically "equivalent" family configurations in fact differ quite substantially and are themselves very heterogeneous: a child can be surrounded by people who represent diverse or even contradictory socialization principles (for example, an illiterate father and a sister at university, or one sibling who is successful at school and another who is not). Lahire emphasizes the fact that the atypical academic success of some of the children in his study was, in part, linked to the presence of contradictory factors, which meant they had at least one member of their family on whom they could rely for support during their schooling.

A similar kind of analysis can be carried out on other atypical school situations (for example when children from highly educated families struggle at school), or more generally with members of white upper-middle class youth on downwardly mobile trajectories. Downward mobility of this kind may seem to call into question the model of the habitus (according to which resources are passed down from one generation to the next). However, observing these trajectories through the lens of a "resource inheritance model of the habitus," Streib has shown that, on the contrary, they confirm the effect of class socialization and the strength with which dispositions are passed on. A sociological approach focusing on socialization can in fact explain downwardly mobile trajectories: in these particular cases of family class socialization, it is "resource weaknesses" that are passed down. These are then exacerbated by internalized identities (also learned and acquired) that consolidate the incomplete transmission of family resources by driving individuals to make a virtue of necessity – for example, the women who learn to see themselves as stay-at-home moms, or the low-income artists and athletes who locate their "purpose, status, and achievements" in pursuing passion rather than money (Streib 2020: 8). Regarding these atypical cases in which transmission of family status does not occur in upper-middle-class families, intra-familial heterogeneity, in particular, can help explain this – as, for example, when a mother with a relatively low level of education spends the most time with the children, whereas the father, who is a college-educated professional and could pass on "high levels of academic skills and institutional know-how," is too hands-off to do so (11).

In explaining why capital is sometimes not passed on, Streib also mentions cases where children cannot "accept and use the resources their parents provided" either because they are not "able" to (and this is her main focus) or because they are not "*willing* to do so" (2020: 150, n. 49). This "acceptance" functions rather like a given constraint or an impenetrable black box, but it is in fact possible to "sociologize" the reception of immaterial inheritance from within the determinist logic of socialization. Mechanisms of reception, appropriation, and negotiation can be analyzed sociologically, not as stumbling blocks or exits from socialization processes, but rather as revealing how behavior is socially determined. A good example can be found in one study of "the modes and conditions under which the children of feminist activists receive, adapt, and negotiate the feminist legacy according to their own biographical experiences, marked by confrontation with a plurality of universes of socialization and contexts in which the inherited dispositions are activated or not" (Masclet 2015: 5). In this case, the family plurality at work is not just that of the parents who pass on different dispositions during the socialization process, but also that of the children – a brother and a sister who do not internalize the same dispositions after being educated by a feminist mother.

3. Variations in childcare arrangements

Intra-familial diversity does not operate automatically but rather, as we have seen, according to "opportunities for socialization." And these are far from limited to the parents alone. From the very earliest age, especially when parents work, childcare may be delegated to other people, whether family or professionals, who are therefore also potential agents of primary socialization: daycare providers who look after one or several children in their own homes, staff in group care settings, babysitters and nannies paid to look after children in the parents' home, or members of the extended family. These different modes of childcare necessarily introduce variation into primary socialization.

The very existence of this principle of variation can be analyzed sociologically. The choice of childcare mode depends in particular on the family's income, professional commitments, and time constraints, but also on their personal preferences, which are shaped by local and global educational norms regarding the "best" choice. The mother's educational attainment (indicative of her class dispositions) plays a big role in this respect, independently of income (which is also obviously important). Less educated mothers tend to prefer family-based care for young children, while more educated mothers tend to prefer certain types of center care that are most closely linked to children's school readiness (Augustine et al. 2009).

"Choice" of childcare therefore depends on a family's social position, which, in terms of primary class socialization, means that the probability that children will come into contact with people from a different social group than their parents varies from one social class to another. Working-class parents are particularly likely either to call upon family members for childcare, which introduces little class variation, or to use certain forms of group care, which can introduce variation because of contact with middle-class professionals with middle-class norms. As for the middle and upper classes, they tend either to use forms of center care staffed by people with middle-class values and aligned with school norms, or paid care at home, where their employees are often working class. The variations in potential agents of primary socialization introduced by childcare can therefore be more or less significant depending on each family's social position and choices. However, sociological studies remain to be designed and conducted to determine whether these diversified contacts result in socialization effects. As mentioned earlier, class hierarchies may well create barriers to socializing effects, especially when it comes to preventing those situated towards the bottom of the social space from having an influence upon those situated towards the top.

4. Childhood professionals and educational norms

The diversity of "socializers" introduced by childcare is part of a broader limitation placed on parental influence by two key actors in childhood socialization: the state and childhood professionals.

Without going as far as the French revolutionary figure Danton, who famously claimed "children belong to the Republic before they belong to their parents," the state's influence as an agent of socialization must nevertheless be taken into account. The state oversees or can even be said to delegate children's primary socialization to families. Its "responsibility" for children's socialization in the family can be seen in the laws that restrict parents' actions and make provision to remove children from the home should their domestic situation be considered a danger to them. Primary socialization is therefore necessarily a matter of concern for the state, which also limits any family monopoly by determining and enforcing the age of compulsory education. In the United States, the introduction of compulsory education prompted conflict, for example in Connecticut where Italian immigrant families "saw schooling as an imposition on the family economy and existing modes of socialization" and "*Padroni* labor recruiters, parents, and young workers themselves placed factory above school" (Schmidt 2013: 182). Such resistance did not last, however, and, as a result, it was ultimately school that became the center of interactions between young people and the state (181), as opposed to the penal system, which was the other institution in a position to play that role.

To some extent, therefore, the state organizes the interactions between the different agents of primary socialization, first and foremost family and school. Moreover, its socializing role is also evident in its oversight of an important category of actors in socialization, namely childhood professionals. As Durkheim put it: "each society, considered at a given stage of development, has a system of education which exercises an irresistible influence on individuals. It is idle to think we can rear our children as we wish" (1956: 65).

Parents are at once "socializers" and themselves "socialized" to the pedagogical work of socialization. However, the people or institutions whose prescriptive norms parents follow vary according to their social position, as we can see in the example of young children's healthcare. For middle-class parents, experts constitute a specific socializing agent, through the books, pamphlets, magazines, and media sources that mothers read, take seriously, and whose precepts they adopt (Bronfenbrenner 1966). In the working classes, rather than following the advice of professional experts, mothers tend instead to take advice from family or peers (lay experts) who serve as agents of socialization to the job of motherhood (Gojard 2010).

As far as childhood professionals are concerned, in addition to their mission of educating children, they also have a mandate to educate families. Today, professionals and researchers working in the fields of psychology and cognition are increasingly involved in this endeavor with parents (Martin 2023). They define the "right" ("healthy," "normal") or "wrong" ("pathological," "deviant") family forms and provide most of the benchmarks and judgments, that is to say the set of norms, that weigh upon families. From this perspective, these professionals can therefore be considered as agents of primary socialization in their own right and sociologists can analyze their practical influence empirically, from various vantage points. The diverse competing norms that exist among professionals can be identified, for instance, as can the differences in those known or put into practice from one family to the next. Most importantly, it is possible to consider the necessary material and *dispositional* conditions for implementing a given norm or the precise effects this will have on family life as well as on children's habits and dispositions.

5. The influence of peers and the cultural industries

Family, childcare providers, and childhood professionals are three categories of socializing agents in which there are distinct differences in status between the socializers and those being socialized. However, the socializing effects of the peer group must also be considered, that is to say the existence of what might be labeled "horizontal" socialization mutually exercised by members of a group in which each individual appears to have the same status.

This influence can be identified at a very early stage and studies in preschool and elementary school settings reveal how the peer group determines children's practices and preferences. Hierarchies are very quickly established according to children's "popularity," with some children perceived, and perceiving themselves, as popular – in other words, admired by others, able to influence them, and possessing the legitimate view within the peer group of what should and should not be done, what is "cool" or not, and so on. These hierarchies form a key component of the "children's society" that develops during primary school and that of course reproduces, but also transposes, aspects of broader society. Attributions of popularity and the resulting hierarchies produce a form of socialization that does not necessarily function according to the same principles as school or family – for example, even in pre-adolescent society, getting good grades can prove an obstacle to popularity among boys and can generate stigma (Adler et al. 1992; Adler and Adler 1998).

It seems that this influence only grows stronger as we move from childhood to adolescence, when "peer culture" has undeniable prescriptive strength and competes with the influence of school and family. Moreover, the norms and models conveyed by popular culture largely circulate through peer culture, and their socializing power is more than likely reinforced by the fact they are borne and represented by the interactions and rules of the real-life social group. Media influence upon the conceptions, attitudes, and practices of children and youths has increased considerably over the last century, to the extent that the media itself has become a "socializing agent [...] in the lives of children and adolescents" and constitutes a space of learning and influence with lasting effects on the individual (Prot et al. 2015). This may mean, as Paul DiMaggio suggests, that socialization is "less experientially based, and more dependent upon media images and hearsay, than many of our theories (for example, Bourdieu's *habitus* construct) imply" (1997: 268). From a sociological perspective, however, this socializing agent should no doubt be studied in relation to those with whom it is discussed and who help frame its influence: parents, where educational programs and websites are concerned, but above all the peer group when it comes to television shows, music, video games, and social networks. This is why, in this subsection, I consider the influence of the peer group and the influence of cultural industries together. A dispositionalist sociology of media socialization remains largely to be constructed with a view to addressing and revising the questions that have long been raised by the sociology of the media about its influence on individual behavior.

Taking into account horizontal socialization should not, however, mean simplifying or overestimating the effect of the peer group. First of all, this form of peer socialization should not be seen as a non-constraining form of socialization or as a non-violent or free form of "self-socialization," as is sometimes argued. Peer socialization does not mean that an individual "socializes themselves" in a way that escapes all social constraint. The prescriptions and influences that emerge from the group within which peer socialization occurs are just as constraining as those present in "vertical" forms of socialization, and the sanctions for deviation can be just as strong. It is important, however, that recognizing this constraint should not overemphasize the effect of the peer group, which is sometimes presented as the sole socializing agent in adolescence. This is far from being the case. For example, Gary Alan Fine's study of socialization processes in little league baseball has shown how close adult–child socialization and peer socialization are in this context, and how the two combine to produce the values, norms, and behaviors internalized by these pre-adolescent boys (Fine 1987).

"Peer cultures" are sometimes described as "autonomous and creative social systems" revolving around two key themes: children "gaining control" over their lives, and children "sharing" that control with others (a perspective explicitly positioned in opposition to the deterministic "reproductive theories of socialization" that I am advocating in this book – an issue I will return to later) (Corsaro and Eder 1990). But are control gain and autonomy, on the one hand, and sharing, on the other, not principles and attitudes that are at least in part inherited from parents and teachers? To borrow an expression from Lahire, one might perhaps more accurately refer to youths as being placed "under triple constraint": that of school, that of parents, and that of peers – or even "quadruple constraint" if we include cultural industries (Lahire 2004). Viewed from this perspective, it is then possible to examine the role of peer socialization in how agents of socialization compete or converge. To return to the different studies mentioned, we can see, for example: how popularity rankings decreed by peer society in American elementary schools borrow criteria from both school society and family social status; how the learning processes involved in sibling play at home in fact perpetuate parental and school socialization, which provides the content of that play and dictates the ways in which one reads a story or interacts with a younger sibling (Gregory 2001); and finally, how mass culture, conveyed by cultural industries or the peer group, can compete with the "cultivated culture" of school (and family, for upper-class youths), thus creating, within the same individual, tastes and practices with varying levels of social legitimacy. Running counter to somewhat idealistic visions of the autonomous and homogeneous nature of "children's society," peer socialization is in fact more an additional constraint than a space of freedom, and it is always a determining form of socialization as opposed to a freely chosen form of self-socialization.

6. School: a hub for primary socialization

Finally, school represents the social space where all the institutions and professionals mentioned in this chapter potentially converge. At school, the family is present in and of itself (in the early years, in particular, parents enter school premises) and also in an embodied form in the child. Childhood professionals, supervised or employed by the state, are also present among teaching, medical, and psychological staff. Lastly, school also serves as a peer-group reservoir. In this respect, it can be argued that even if the family to some extent controls or filters other socializing influences such as peers, the media, and professionals (Lahire 2013: 124), it is nevertheless school that serves as the hub for primary socialization. It is both a specific institution of socialization and a space in which other forms of socialization are encountered and interconnect. It is sometimes even responsible for assessing the products of other agents of socialization, for example, family socialization, which often comes under close scrutiny when children "fail" or behave "badly" at school.

However, the school's particular position among institutions of socialization is also a result of other factors. The strength and importance of school socialization is first and foremost a result of its duration. Since early childhood became viewed as a locus for pedagogical work (Chamboredon and Prévot 1975), school socialization has preceded compulsory schooling insofar as most children now attend preschool. In most cases, therefore, school socialization extends from the preschool years through to the end of high school. Plural primary socialization is established from a very early age and educational establishments hold pride of place within that multi-faceted configuration. We shall look at a few empirical examples illustrating this, from the beginning and the end of the school career (socialization in higher education will be addressed in the next chapter, along with professional socialization).

Karin Martin has shown that school socialization affects gender incorporation from as early as preschool, arguing that the latter's "hidden curriculum" "turns children who are similar in bodily comportment, movement, and practice into girls and boys – children whose bodily practices differ" through "five sets of practices": "dressing up, permitting relaxed behaviors or requiring formal behaviors, controlling voices, verbal and physical instructions regarding children's bodies by teachers, and physical interactions among children." School socialization therefore produces two major products: it "creates bodily differences between the genders" and it naturalizes these differences, making them "appear and feel natural" (Martin 1998: 494). The later middle-school socialization processes studied by Michela Musto (and in particular educators' differential responses to boys' rule-breaking) show how school continues to shape students' gender-status beliefs vis-à-vis perceptions of intelligence, and in particular contributes to the gendered social construction of (masculine) exceptionalism, thus reproducing social inequalities in early adolescence (Musto 2019). In this respect, school follows on from the family socialization we saw in the previous chapter – with the visit to the zoo for example – and we can begin to see how gender socialization is particularly prone to progressive construction from one agent to the next.

Analyzing school socialization therefore also means considering the extent to which the different processes making up plural primary socialization reinforce one another or, conversely, clash and compete. One of the main tools through which school socialization operates is written and spoken language, which is a fundamental product of family class socialization. Depending on the social position of their family, children will use and relate to language in ways that are more or less congruent with its use at school, which fosters a written, reflexive, and distanced relationship towards it. The analyses provided by Lahire and his research team on the *Enfances de classe* project (2019) foreground the diversity of linguistic class socialization, which has long been studied by sociology and linguistics. The study shows how working-class linguistic socialization produces a pragmatic relationship to language among children, as a result of which they tend to use it only as it reflects experience and structures situations, when its meaning and function are clear. They typically do not see the value of the linguistic precision demanded at school, of subtle semantic distinctions, or of reflexive word play. Different children will therefore have unequal relationships to the language required in the school setting, and their family linguistic socialization means they are not equally equipped to succeed academically. Moreover, school socialization, which operates via language, will therefore be more or less successful depending on these varying relationships to language and the extent to which the students' class-based linguistic dispositions are compatible with it.

An ethnographic study conducted by Jessica Calarco with students in a public elementary school also offers a way of considering the question of plural socialization, particularly in the shape of the "encounter" between family and school socialization. Different types of class socialization produce different children who, for example, interact differently with their teachers. Middle-class children tend to "negotiate advantages" by asking for more assistance, accommodation, and attention from their teachers. This, in turn, leads to different and unequal forms of school socialization, feelings and attitudes towards school, and trajectories within the institution. The children progressively internalize the "lessons" of this socialization between the third and the seventh grade, to the extent that differences in class attitudes become more pronounced during elementary school (Calarco 2018). From a very early age, there is a correlation between school rankings (which children are "best" at doing their "job" as students from the institution's point of view, but also which parents are best at doing their job as parents) (Lareau and Calarco 2012) and social class: from the very earliest stages of children's schooling, the different forms of class socialization are not equivalent in the eyes of the school.

School thus serves as what Lahire qualifies as an apparatus (*dispositif* in French) of socialization, that is to say a "relatively coherent set of discursive and non-discursive practices, of objects, and of machines" that contribute to "making" a particular type of individual (2005: 323). As such, it extends far beyond teacher–student interactions and the classroom. School socialization begins, as we have just seen, when children are as young as two or three and continues throughout their childhood and adolescence, and even beyond high school.

America's elite boarding schools, for example, studied by Peter Cookson and Caroline Persell in the 1980s, "were created to mold and shape adolescents in a particular way" and to "prepare for power" those who have to learn the "habit of command" through the institution's explicit education but also through processes of peer socialization that, at first glance, might seem unrelated (Cookson and Persell 1985). Shamus Khan's 2011 study of a prep school he refers to as "St. Paul's" shows that specific processes of socialization are still at work among the socially privileged youths who attend elite boarding schools. In terms of academic learning, what students acquire is not so much content as a relationship to knowledge: they learn to have confidence in the legitimacy of their personal point of view and are encouraged to consider their homework assignments as contributions to general academic knowledge on a given topic. The students come to believe they are "something special" (Kahn 2011: 160) and that they deserve the treatment they receive – living and working at St Paul's, listening to famous speakers who have come especially to give a talk for them, flying to New York for a day to go to an opera, and so on – while at the same time experiencing all this privilege as something banal. Their "persistent indifference to extraordinary things" (185) is itself a manifestation of the "ease of privilege" (77) prevalent among these privileged adolescents – the product of both the family socialization that formed them and the school socialization of the particular institution they are attending.

The results of school socialization are, indeed, far from limited to the purely academic sphere and affect some more surprising practices, such as attire. In the case of St. Paul's, the students attend bi-weekly seated dinners with faculty in formal dress, learning to feel at ease in such social occasions and to consider them routine (with the young girls, for example, learning to wear often revealing formal clothing as a way of both respecting and challenging the rules [Kahn 2011: 123–5]). In a very different case, in the predominately minority, urban middle school studied by Edward Morris, a form of bodily discipline is exercised over behavior and dress (although not necessarily effectively incorporated), with

African American girls admonished for not being "lady-like" enough and Latino boys instructed to "tuck in that shirt." As Morris puts it, "schools teach children many lessons. These lessons often transgress the formal elements of overt curricula and instruct children how to speak, what to wear, how to move their bodies, and, ultimately, how to inhabit different race, class, and gender positions" (2005: 44). Through this training in how to dress, both Khan's and Morris's examples show that, beyond addressing the practical question of visible dress codes, the school socialization that takes place also serves as socialization to the social order and to class, gender, and race relations and the students' position within those relations. In the prep school, this leads to entitled merit being justified and naturalized, while in the middle school it sometimes produces alienation from schooling.

In terms of its products, school socialization therefore involves three main types of learning. First, it is the place where the academic content and skills outlined in textbooks and curricula are acquired. As with all types of socialization, though, as well as this explicit educational dimension there is also an implicit dimension made up of more diffuse and less immediately visible learning processes. These relate to a certain relationship to time and space (through timetables, school buildings, etc.), to particular uses of the body, as we have just seen, and more generally to the social order and one's place in it. Finally, to these dimensions of school socialization, it is important also to add everything that is learned either at the margins of the institution (e.g. peer socialization to romance or culture) or even running counter to its tenets (e.g. how to "cheat" during a test, get away with smoking, or think about other things while pretending to pay attention in class).

School is thus a hub for childhood and teenage socialization, and an institution that today exerts an especially long, continuous influence on the individual. Its particular role is the result of a set of historical transformations that have made school socialization into the dominant mode of socialization through which we are formed – a mode characterized, in particular, by the constitution of a separate childhood universe, the importance of rules in learning, rational time management, and a plethora of exercises that are an end in themselves (Vincent et al. 1994; Darmon 2020). This historical process is not simply about the fact that education lasts longer or that protracted school trajectories have been potentially extended to all social classes; it also relates to the ways in which the model of school socialization has been disseminated in fairly distant social worlds, for example in after-school activities, sports, social work, company training programs or team-building activities, and even certain television programs, such as competitive singing or cooking shows. All educational processes today seem to be "prisoners of the school form" (Vincent et al. 1994) and it is as if all social experiences were supposed to be educational and an opportunity to teach or to learn something.

As a consequence, certain areas of practice and institutions that are not related to school per se draw upon skills acquired during school socialization (sometimes almost invisibly or unconsciously) and thus favor those who have had a long education and/or who have acquired dispositions close to this school form within their families. Such phenomena can explain some of the social inequalities present in an area as removed from school as, for example, post brain-stroke rehabilitation centers: "the 'school form of the hospital' proves far more efficient with patients who have scholastic dispositions" and can "explain the class-based processes through which health inequalities arise" (Darmon 2020: 235). We saw earlier how school socialization can focus on non-academic areas such as clothing or the relationship to the social world. Similarly, in this context, we can see how skills and practices that, in theory, seem quite distant from the school institution (mastering cognitive games or exercises, using written plans to compensate for deficient memory, or utilizing drawings to learn to walk again) are in fact closely linked to it. This process operates through the hospital's treatment plan (its "curriculum," as it were) and the work accomplished not by teachers, in this instance, but by professionals such as physical therapists, speech-and-language therapists, and neuropsychologists. This reveals both the unique position that school occupies in primary socialization and also its strength that is sometimes masked by family socialization, which seems more self-evident and is perhaps more immediately visible.

If primary socialization is so strong (and if its products are so persistent), this is therefore not because it is homogeneous nor because family socialization has an exclusive monopoly on it – a hypothesis that this chapter has tried to show is somewhat unlikely. An individual's initial experiences and learning processes produce persisting effects throughout the life course despite – or perhaps *thanks to* – the multiple agents that make up primary socialization. It remains important, of course, not to neglect the specific role and effects of family socialization. While school may be a "hub" for primary socialization, the family remains a key "actor" in plural primary socialization, because, unlike the other agents of socialization, it is in a position to act upon all the socializing influences in play. It can, for example, to some extent control access to the media or the peer group, whether directly or through the choice of neighborhood or school, and this is especially true among the upper-middle classes (Kosunen and Rivière 2018; Authier and Lehman-Frisch 2015).

Finally, these possibilities of playing on multiplicity raise the question of *variations in multiplicity itself*. The diverse range of potential agents of socialization pointed us to the plural nature of primary socialization, but, as we have seen, this plurality itself can vary according to identifiable social factors. Chamboredon put forward this very hypothesis in a 1971 article in which he argued that the privileged classes are distinguished by their disposition to regulate and control areas of conduct ("not only work, but also controlling emotions, learning techniques of sociability, sexuality, etc.") that, in working-class families, would be open to the influence of the peer group (Chamboredon 2015: 99). It is likely, for example, that relative time spent with family members or with the peer group will correspond to identifiable social positions, as we saw earlier in the case of the children studied by Lareau, who drew a distinction between the working classes and the upper-middle classes in this regard. Mechanisms and strategies for creating coherency from plural influences may also be used, for example when parents monitor social interactions or media consumption, but also when they choose modes of childcare (e.g. when the working classes tend to call on family members). Identifying the diverse range of agents involved in primary socialization is only one part of the necessary sociological work. Once that is done, we must then look to real-life situations and consider how these agents compete or cohere, that is to say the extent to which plural socialization is actually effective. Are the forms of primary socialization that take place at each extreme of the social scale more coherent than the others? Some of the studies I have presented here may give the impression that there is greater homogeneity in primary socialization at the two ends of the spectrum of social class. However, the material conditions of existence inherent to childhood and youth – placing both under a "triple constraint" – nevertheless mean that heterogeneous situations are still more than probable, with "the school obligation necessarily creating cultural dissonance" among working-class youths, and the media and cultural industries playing an equivalent role in relation to the upper classes (Lahire 2004: 497–556).

The plural nature of primary socialization is therefore both an observation, resulting from the examination of primary socialization in our societies, and a problem, that is to say a starting point for numerous avenues of research. It is necessary to consider the relationships between its different forms but also to examine how these, in turn, intersect with other processes of socialization that take place after the childhood and teenage years. This is the topic explored in the next chapter.

3
Rebuilding People: The Varied Forms of Secondary Socialization

"The first five years of your child's life are the most important years – the formative years." This statement is taken from Fitzhugh Dodson's 1970 bestseller *How to Parent*, a work sometimes cited to caricature approaches in which only primary socialization seems to matter. If such approaches were accurate, this book could have ended after the first two chapters, since it would mean that the socialization process ended with childhood and that the rest of the life cycle was nothing more than the non-problematic actualization of everything previously internalized. But just as socialization does not only take place in the family, so it is not only primary, and not everything is defined in childhood (even within a sociology of socialization that ascribes considerable influence to it). Simply negating that idea does not, however, tell us very much about exactly what happens after primary socialization and how.

Answering this question means examining the forms of socialization that are labeled "adult" or "secondary." These qualifiers indicate that sociologists have analyzed other agents of socialization than those discussed in the first two chapters, and other moments of socialization than childhood, and have concluded that they play an important role in constructing and shaping individuals. The expressions, especially "secondary socialization," also emphasize a both self-evident and fundamental characteristic of these forms of socialization: they occur "after" or "subsequently." Whereas primary socialization builds the individual from their very first days of existence, the starting point for secondary socialization is very different. It neither "creates" nor "produces" a social being *ex nihilo* but instead must somehow deal with the previously incorporated products of primary socialization that have made the individual into the person they have become. Secondary socialization is therefore necessarily a process of *reconstruction*, and one of the issues at stake in analyzing it is to understand how it interacts with primary socialization.

I begin here by defining secondary socialization and considering the problems posed by its relationship with primary socialization. I then focus on one ideal-type: the professional socialization of doctors, illustrating the competing approaches to this question proposed by functionalist and interactionist sociologists. Finally, taking into account the fact that secondary socialization is far from limited to professional socialization, I provide an overview of other examples that reveal both its diversity and its variable links with primary socialization.

1. Defining secondary socialization

It has sometimes been argued that one of the main contributions of Peter Berger and Thomas Luckmann's now classic 1966 book on theories of socialization, *The Social Construction of Reality*, resides in the supposedly novel distinction it introduced between primary and secondary socialization. However, as the authors themselves state, their definitions of socialization and its two subtypes, primary and secondary, "closely follow current usages in the social sciences" (1991: 229).[4] It could instead be argued that the book's main value lies in the way it *problematized* the relationship and interconnections between primary and secondary socialization.

1.1 Primary socialization: strength and affectivity

In order to offer an account of this, it is necessary first to return briefly to primary socialization, which Berger and

Luckmann define in terms inspired by the psychological approach of the early twentieth-century philosopher George Herbert Mead, from whom they borrowed in particular the expressions "generalized other" and "significant other" (Mead 1934). A "significant other" is a person physically and emotionally present in the child's surroundings who is very important to the child and who will influence their behavior and how they view themselves. The current use of this term to refer to a romantic partner might therefore seem quite distant from this definition but, as we shall see later when we look at marital socialization, this is not necessarily the case!

From this perspective, children's relationships with their significant others mark them in a lasting fashion insofar as, initially, they only perceive themselves through the points of view and actions of those people. It is also important to note that Berger and Luckmann do not limit themselves to what they term the "socio-psychological" approach that only takes into account the internalization of roles and attitudes of others: in their view, what is internalized is, more precisely, the "world" of significant others – a specific social world, for example that of a particular social class.

In a second stage, the circle of people who help construct the child progressively expands and becomes a "generalized other." Berger and Luckmann illustrate this aspect of primary socialization as follows:

> For example, in the internalization of norms there is a progression from, "Mummy is angry with me *now*" to, "Mummy is angry with me *whenever* I spill the soup." As additional significant others (father, grandmother, older sister, and so on) support the mother's negative attitude towards soup-spilling, the generality of the norm is subjectively extended. The decisive step comes when the child recognizes that everybody is against soup-spilling, and the norm is generalized to, "One does not spill soup" – "one" being himself as part of a generality that includes, in principle, all of society in so far as it is significant to the child. (1991: 152–3)

Drawing on this approach to primary socialization, Berger and Luckmann identify certain features that then allow them, by differentiation, to define secondary socialization. First of all, primary socialization is particularly strong and persistent. It possesses a "peculiar quality of firmness" (155) that makes it "the most important [socialization] for an individual" (151) and that explains why its effects persist throughout the life course, insofar as the world that the child internalizes is "deeply rooted in consciousness" (167). Secondly, because of the nature of the relationships between children and their significant others, primary socialization is necessarily embedded in an affective context that is "highly charged emotionally" (151).

1.2 The bureaucratic worlds of secondary socialization

As defined by Berger and Luckmann, primary socialization is "the first socialization an individual undergoes in childhood," while secondary socialization is "any subsequent process that inducts an already socialized individual into new sectors of the objective world of his society" (1991: 150). This fairly general definition is quickly specified with reference to the "division of labour" and becomes "the internalization of institutional or institution-based 'sub-worlds'" and "the acquisition of role specific knowledge, the roles being directly or indirectly rooted in the division of labour" (158). Here the authors follow on from a tendency that preceded them and has continued after them consisting in more or less equating the notion of secondary socialization with that of professional socialization, or at the very least placing professional socialization at the heart of secondary socialization. The examples they use to illustrate secondary socialization are almost all drawn from two areas: the world of work and the world of school viewed as preparation for the world of work.

Two characteristics of secondary socialization follow from this definition, each corresponding to those of primary socialization. Where primary socialization is strong and affective, secondary socialization is defined relatively and in the negative as less strong and less affective – in a sense, almost bureaucratic. To begin with the latter point, Berger and Luckmann argue that secondary socialization can "dispense" with "emotionally charged identification" because "it is necessary to love one's mother, but not one's teacher" (1991: 161). Defined in this way, the agents of secondary socialization hold roles and positions that others could hold in their stead: a given piece of knowledge could be taught by one teacher or another, just as a given "trick of the trade" could be passed on by different colleagues. From this perspective, to paraphrase Max Weber's famous typology, it could be argued that primary socialization's effectiveness is based on traditional and quasi-charismatic authority, whereas secondary socialization draws its power from legal-rational authority. The two types of socialization are also different in another respect: secondary socialization is less pervasive. As we saw in the first chapter, children internalize the family world as the only world, "the world *tout court*," whereas adults internalize the world of work in a more situated and relative fashion, inhabiting it as one world among others. The socialization process will therefore not result in its products becoming "rooted" in the individual in the same way. Berger and Luckmann emphasize that unlike the results of primary socialization, which are very difficult to "disintegrate" (162), the results of secondary socialization are much more vulnerable to destruction. One of the examples given by the authors is tie-wearing. If a man has taken for granted, during his professional socialization, that he must wear a tie to work, only a small structural change will be required for him to give up this practice – for example, if he changes job or company and the dress code is different. Going "against" this product of his secondary socialization will not clash with anything deeply rooted within him. On the other hand, Berger and Luckmann argue, a very deep conversion would be necessary for him to go to work wearing no clothes whatsoever, illustrating the far stronger passive "resistance" (to use Durkheim's term for the manifestation of social facts) of the products of primary socialization, which has taught us to be naked in front of other people in only very specific situations.

Not only do Berger and Luckmann provide criteria for differentiating between primary and secondary socialization, they also offer some ways to move beyond the overly stark contrasts of the distinction (the "warm" maternal world of primary socialization, realm of the passions, as opposed to the "cold" bureaucratic world of salaried work, where emotion has no place and reason alone governs what is internalized). They argue that certain secondary socialization processes can "resemble" primary socialization, in terms both of how pervasive they are and of their affective dimension – particularly when institutions with an interest in this kind of secondary socialization use certain techniques explicitly with a view to producing, for example, priests, revolutionaries, or musicians who are entirely dedicated to their vocation. It is not certain, however, that secondary socialization only has an emotional side in such extreme cases. Certain occupations, particularly in the service sector, are the space and matrix for a particular form of secondary socialization that consists precisely in "emotion work" – learning to feel or manage emotions in a particular way – and we will come back to this later (Hochschild 2012).

1.3 The relationship between primary and secondary socialization

Berger and Luckmann do not, however, simply define these two subtypes of socialization. One of the major contributions of their approach resides in the way they frame the question of the relationship between primary and secondary socialization as a problem rather than as something self-evident. Because primary socialization is so powerful and its products are so firmly "rooted" in the individual, how is it even possible for anything to come afterwards, that is to say later forms of socialization? How does secondary socialization "deal with" the prior contents of primary socialization? Unlike in Chapters 1 and 2, the problem is no longer understanding the links between plural and largely concomitant socialization processes, but rather considering the temporal dynamics of diverse, successive processes. For Berger and Luckmann, the question of "the consistency between the original and the new internalizations" is "fundamental," especially the fact that secondary socialization "must deal with an already formed self and an already internalized world" (1991: 160). To illustrate the idea that secondary socialization "cannot construct subjective reality ex nihilo" and that it must be analyzed on the basis of primary socialization, the authors use the example of foreign-language learning. We learn a second language (a metaphor for secondary socialization) "by building on the taken-for-granted reality of one's 'mother tongue'" (163) (a metaphor for primary socialization), and, for a long time, we translate elements of the new language into the old language. As time passes, if we learn and use the language in a sustained enough fashion, it gradually becomes possible to "think" directly in the new language, but it is rare to attain levels of ease equivalent to those we have in our first language. From this point of view, the situation of a child raised bilingually, who learns both languages at the same time, is no doubt different, and the authors' metaphor shows that analyses of secondary socialization cannot avoid the issue of the temporal sequence of socialization processes and the way in which their contents are interconnected.

2. How a doctor is made: a "historical" example of professional socialization

As we have seen, in *The Social Construction of Reality* secondary socialization is very quickly equated with one form or other of professional socialization, and the latter is viewed above all as a *training* process that engages school as well as the world of work. In this respect, Berger and Luckmann's work reflects relatively common tendencies in sociology, in which it often seems self-evident that studying secondary socialization means answering the following question: how, and to what extent, do professional training (including at school) and the world of work construct the individual anew? The example of secondary socialization on which I focus here – medical socialization and the process through which individuals "become" doctors – is also part of this analytical inclination. In many ways, the example constitutes a "dual ideal-type" of secondary socialization in its capacity as both professional socialization and socialization to the medical profession – an area that, in American sociology, has traditionally been used as a typical case through which to study the professions in general. Furthermore, the many years of medical training bring up the question of how academic training (at university) interconnects with quasi-professional training (as an intern in a hospital), which we have already seen is central in many sociological approaches to secondary socialization.

Finally, focusing on the socialization of young doctors is warranted in particular by how important this subject of study has been in the history of sociology. As well as representing a scientific topic of inquiry, it was the battleground for a clash between two sociological traditions: functionalism and interactionism. At exactly the same time, Robert Merton, from Columbia University, and Everett Hughes, from the University of Chicago, launched and directed two competing studies of this socialization process. The scene is 1950s America: reading the two books, one can almost imagine the background music to *The Godfather* accompanying a split screen showing two rival gangs and chronicling their preparations, their altercations, and their results! The two research teams' interest in this particular topic was guided by the same aim: analyzing medical students as "prototypes" – a term they both used – allowing the study of professional socialization. However, for Hughes and his researchers, it was also a way of showing how fruitful the interactionist approach could be and of demonstrating its superiority, especially in methodological terms, over functionalist approaches to the professions (Chapoulie 2020: 182–3). The following section looks at the aspects of these studies and their multi-faceted competition that concern socialization.

2.1 *The Student-Physician*: medical culture and anticipatory socialization

The study directed by Robert Merton (1957: esp. 3–79) was explicitly part of what he referred to at the time as the "growth of interest in the process of adult socialization." For a long time, analysis of socialization had been limited to its family dimensions, but Merton suggested it was now time to consider socialization as a continuous process throughout the life course. For this particular study, this meant considering "the processes by which the neophyte is transformed into one or another kind of medical man" (Merton et al. 1957: 52) during medical studies, and considering medical school itself as "a social environment in which the professional culture of medicine is variously transmitted to novices through distinctive social and psychological processes" (vii).

The Student-Physician's focus on the academic side of learning the profession does not, however, mean that it overemphasizes "education" to the detriment of more implicit forms of socialization. Merton gives great emphasis to a point mentioned earlier regarding the distinction between socialization and education, namely the importance of what he calls "indirect learning" during which "attitudes, values, and behavior patterns are acquired as byproducts of contact with instructors and peers, with patients, and with members of the health team" (41) whom the students encounter throughout their education and years of internships in hospitals.

2.1.1 Learning to reconcile contradictory norms

Merton argues that the medical socialization process ultimately results in a capacity to blend together the potentially contradictory norms of medical culture. He defines medical culture as a set of norms that are shared and passed on, and according to which physicians are supposed to determine their actions. It therefore sets out a realm of possibilities, both technical and moral, determining which behaviors are prescribed, preferred, allowed, or prohibited, thus codifying the values of the profession. However, this system of values is organized in such a way that, for each norm, there exists another one that is sufficiently different for a delicate balancing act to be required in order to respect them both. Merton gives a list of twenty-one dual injunctions that define the medical role; for example, a physician must "keep pace" with the latest advances in medical knowledge, but must make as much time as possible "for the care of his patients"; he must not become "overly identified with patients," but he must show them "compassionate concern"; he must "collaborate" with his team "rather than dominate them," but equally "he has final responsibility" for their actions (Merton et al. 1957: 73–5). The "function" of medical socialization thus becomes to teach students how to turn a normative system of potentially incompatible components into an efficient, coherent, and stable guide for professional conduct.

As we shall see, this aspect of the functionalist approach was strongly criticized by interactionists for both its *a priori* and its *ex post* dimensions. Where the former is concerned, the table of medical values was essentially decreed by Merton. Regarding the latter, the socialization process was analyzed from the point of view of its end, that is to say both its *ending* (the result of becoming a doctor is posited, the necessary steps to achieve this are deduced, and only then are empirical illustrations sought) and its *aim* (the process is envisaged as, in part, normative: the intention is to find out how "good" or "experienced" doctors are produced). We can see here, in a more developed form, a stance we encountered earlier regarding primary socialization in the work of Durkheim and above all Parsons.

2.1.2 Finalism and socialization by the reference group

This *finalism* is theorized within the functionalist concept of socialization itself through the notion of "anticipatory socialization" developed by Merton in another text (Merton and Rossi 1968). In *The Student-Physician*, he defined socialization as the set of processes through which individuals acquire "the values and attitudes, the interests, skills, and knowledge – in short, the culture – current in the groups of which they are, *or seek to become* [my emphasis], a member." (Merton et al. 1957: 287)

The individuals being socialized are therefore subjected to the influence of the medical profession into which they will later be admitted, and not only that of their teachers or classmates. In a text reexamining data from a large study on American soldiers during World War II, Merton theorized the notion of "anticipatory socialization" in which an individual is socialized to the group to which he wishes to, but does not yet, belong (Merton and Rossi 1968). Merton shows that certain recruits display values (conformity with army control) that are not those of their "membership group" (that is, the soldiers, many of whom view army control as too strict and see those who respect it too rigidly as "brown-nosers") but those of the group that provides their frame of reference (labeled the "reference group") and whose ranks they aspire to join (that is, the military institution and hierarchy). The soldiers who have undergone anticipatory socialization are the ones with the most chance of being promoted. For Merton, adopting the values of the reference group is a factor in mobility towards that group, providing that the social system is not too rigid. Although Merton expands upon the varied functions and consequences of anticipatory socialization for soldiers, the army, and society, he does not say much about the mechanisms through which the internalization takes place: Does wishing to be socialized suffice in order to become socialized? How does socialization operate in the absence of prolonged contact with the reference group, insofar as the individual is, by definition, not yet a member? These questions can also be applied to the field of medical socialization, in which the end (becoming an experienced physician) is such a given that it almost entirely overwrites the mechanisms that lead to it – and yet these warrant detailed examination. They are precisely what lie at the heart of interactionist analysis.

2.2 *Boys in White*: student culture and socialization by situation

Whereas the functionalists gave equal importance to primary and secondary socialization, interactionist studies focused much more on secondary socialization. In doing so, they ascribed to it many of the features and processes that characterized primary socialization. The founding text by Everett Hughes, "The Making of a Physician" (1956), offers a good illustration of this. Hughes defines medical socialization as "a set of planned and unplanned experiences by which laymen, usually young and acquainted with the prevailing lay medical culture, become possessed of some part of the technical and scientific medical culture of the professionals" (1956: 22).

2.2.1 *The making of a physician: a research program*

In this text, Hughes uses the notion of "significant others" to refer to the people who are particularly important in an individual's secondary socialization. In using the term, he does more than simply borrow it from Mead's theory of primary socialization. Hughes argues that, in secondary socialization, "significant others" are both diverse (for a future physician, they can be colleagues, superiors, teachers, or patients) and variable (the people who play this role change over time and according to the situation). Significant others are not rare; on the contrary, there are a great many of them, creating shifting "configurations" of significant others throughout secondary socialization. Compared to Berger and Luckmann's analysis, in which primary socialization is defined by the presence of significant others and secondary socialization by their absence, we can see that Hughes's earlier text suggests a different criterion for differentiating between the two types of socialization: secondary socialization is, according to him, characterized by the greater diversity of and variation in significant others.

Hughes presents secondary socialization as a reconstruction, or even a transformation, and this is encapsulated in his definition of medical socialization as making "laymen" possessed of "lay medical culture" (that of their area or cultural zone, for example) into people who possess a professional culture. Hughes characterizes this transformation with the famous image of a "passing through the mirror" that "consists of a separation, almost an alienation, of the student from the lay medical world" (1956: 22) in which they begin to see the world from the other side of the mirror and are converted to the professional's reverse view.

In order to offer an account of professional socialization, what must therefore be analyzed is how this initiation unfolds and the resulting conversion processes. The study directed by Hughes, which gave rise to the book *Boys in White* (Becker et al. 1992), was conducted in this vein.

2.2.2 The anti-functionalism of Boys in White

The study's main research question evolved over the course of both the investigation and the book. While its starting point was studying "boys becoming medical men" (Becker et al. 1992: 3), and examining "what medical school did to medical students other than giving them a technical education" (17), in the end, the issue addressed by the book was the "level and direction" of students' efforts. In other words, it asked what the *students* did collectively to the institution (in the double sense of "what are their actions within the institution?" and "to what extent do these actions shape the institution"?). As the subtitle of the book, "Student culture in medical culture" suggests, the authors went from analyzing "medical culture" to studying "student culture" (and, as we shall see, analyzing the socializing effects of this specific student condition).

Both this evolution and its final end point constituted a criticism of the functionalist approach to medical socialization, which was Hughes's intention. From an epistemological point of view, the authors of *Boys in White* reproached functionalists for the "speculative" nature of their analysis, particularly for their tendency to make key "assumptions" regarding matters about which they in fact knew nothing, such as the "medical role" that was allegedly internalized during medical socialization but that no empirical study could determine – for example, the table of medical values drawn up by Merton. How can one claim that students internalize what they need in order to play the role of physician if one knows nothing about that role? The authors of *Boys in White* asserted their preference for an open theoretical framework in which the variables themselves had to be identified, as opposed to an approach in which pre-determined variables are identified and their consequences isolated and measured. In *Boys in White*, the interactionists were therefore quick to *avoid* positing two central elements: (1) the guidelines a physician needs in order to act (because only a study looking at doctors' daily practices could provide this information); (2) what the students learn during their education (on the contrary, one of the key aims of the research was to identify the content and modes of student learning).

Several fundamental criticisms result from this initial point: what happens during medical training cannot be reduced to the question of "becoming a physician." The young people who enter medical school (at the time of *Boys in White*, they were overwhelmingly young men) do not magically become "medical men" once they have completed their training, and they must first learn to become "medical students" – something to which they are driven by both the institution (which never fails to remind them of the fact they are not yet physicians, even during their internships in hospitals) and their situation. In order to describe how the students experience this situation, the authors of *Boys in White* use a metaphor:

> How to climb the distant mountain [the functionalists' "becoming a physician"] may be a question in the backs of their heads; how to make their way across the swamp they

are floundering in now [their workload] and over the steep hill just ahead [the first semester examinations] engages their immediate attention. (Becker et al. 1992: 5)

Boys in White is therefore not a study of "becoming a physician." That does not mean, however, that the book is not a study of secondary socialization. From its authors' perspective, professional education and training institutions clearly produce particular types of people. The students participate in shaping themselves via the institution and seek to be shaped by it. But this process of construction is far from simple, automatic, and unequivocal, and it cannot be reduced to the "internalization of the medical role." The students do not simply become what the medical school wants them to become, nor do they become what is written in the university's brochures. More generally, this approach reminds us that the effective results of socialization must not be confused with the official aims or the intentions of a socializing agent. The approach provides a conception of socialization that, in all respects, stands in opposition to the functionalist theory: it is student socialization (becoming-a-medical-student) not professional socialization; it is as horizontal as it is vertical, thanks to the influence of the peer group; it is relative to a given situation, not determined by the institution's aims; it is studied in action, not on the basis of pre-established or presupposed results; thus, it is descriptive and analytical, not normative. We shall now look at this in more detail by examining the products of this socialization, or what the authors call "perspectives."

2.2.3 "Perspectives" as the products of socialization

The authors borrow the term "perspective" from Mead's philosophy of action, in which it refers to the perceptions and action plans that individuals follow in problematic situations. Reading *Boys in White* in light of everything examined so far in this book, the authors' use of the term could be interpreted as referring to the product of a socialization process.

Perspectives are all at once "a co-ordinated set of ideas and actions a person uses in dealing with some problematic situation," the person's "ordinary way of thinking and feeling about and acting in such a situation," and "the matrix through which one perceives his environment" (Becker et al. 1992: 34) (the authors borrow the latter two expressions from other texts). An important point to note is that these perspectives are not just "ideas" or "conceptions" of the situation (as the term might seem to suggest) but include representations and practices, formed and learned by individuals in response to a specific set of institutional pressures, the immediate context of which must be reconstituted in order for them to be understood. A perspective is therefore made up of several elements: a definition of the situation in which the actors are caught up, the existence of aims or targets towards which the action is directed, a set of ideas about which practices would be profitable or appropriate, and a set of activities or practices that are coherent with these representations.

The evolution of students' perspectives during the first year of medicine illustrates how certain perspectives are learned progressively (chapters 5 to 10 of *Boys in White*). When they arrive, all students face one key, pressing problem: work overload, that is, the astronomical amount of things to learn and the lack of information about what they are supposed to know. The theoretical and practical problem facing the students is that of the "level and direction" of their efforts. In order to respond, again theoretically and practically, to this problem, the student group develops three distinct perspectives, one after the other, as ways of handling it. The first perspective, which the authors show is shared by all students, consists in making "an effort 'to learn it all.'" During this initial period, from the beginning of their studies to their first examinations, the students are entirely caught up in this endeavor: they work constantly, their dreams reflect their academic work, and their jokes revolve around it too ("It's only Monday and I'm behind already").

In the second stage, examinations and an increase in effective interactions between students (especially discussions about work) lead to a new perspective being established, which the authors label "provisional": "You can't do it all" no matter how hard you try. It therefore becomes important to find "the most effective and economical ways" of studying and a criterion for selecting the "things that are important." Unlike the initial perspective, this one subdivides the students into two contrasting groups that diverge when it comes to what criterion to adopt. The first group decides "whether something is important according to whether it is important in medical practice" and the question underpinning their perspective is "Will I have to know about this when I am in practice?" The second group decides "whether something is important according to whether it is what the faculty wants us to know" and asks "How can I find out what the faculty wants us to know?" The two groups do not form by chance. The group that quickly directs its efforts towards faculty expectations is made up of members of the main fraternities (who therefore live together, eat together, and belong to a shared community). The students who do not belong to a fraternity, on the other hand, are undecided about which criterion to choose and eventually choose relevance to future medical practice. The authors take this analysis further and identify the reasons why the "fraternity men" adopt the "faculty expectations" perspective. First, they note the influence of a conception of university linked to the social position of these young people, who are from more educated, higher-class backgrounds than their classmates. Moreover, these students have belonged to fraternities for several years and developed the collective habit of working by anticipating faculty requirements and finding the appropriate techniques to meet them. Finally, their many interactions, linked to communal life and work, reactivate these past skills and explain why the perspective becomes established in the group very quickly (and why the opposite perspective takes much longer to take root in a group that is not as close-knit and has fewer interactions).

This provisional situation, in which the class is divided into two groups with different, competing perspectives, does not last long. Once the first semester examinations are over, the interactions between all the students increase considerably, in part because there is more lab work, which brings the "independents" closer to the "fraternity men." This situation fosters the emergence of a common perspective within the whole class. Given the dominant position of the fraternity group (produced in general by their higher social position and more specifically by their greater, more visible success in the examinations), their perspective and selection criteria become established among all the students. The fraternity men's provisional perspective becomes the "final perspective" that directs the actions of the whole class until the end of the year: learning "what they want us to know."

2.2.4 Primary and secondary socialization

This example of the genesis and transformation of perspectives allows us to return to the question of the relationship between primary and secondary socialization. Despite the emphasis that the interactionists give to secondary socialization, from their point of view the products of prior socialization are neither discredited nor destroyed by secondary socialization, which does not take place in a social vacuum but is exercised upon individuals who already have "perspectives." Hughes had already expressed this idea, in different terms, in his programmatic text: "The period of initiation into the role appears to be one wherein the two cultures, lay and professional, interact within the individual" (1956: 22). From this point of view, *Boys in White* theorizes how perspectives emerge and stabilize: new perspectives appear when the situation requires it; that is, when prior perspectives (those born from primary socialization) are incapable of guiding behavior in a situation that is "problematic," unprecedented, and requires an action or a choice. More often than not, an individual will act according to previously internalized perspectives; it is only when the situation and the prior perspectives are incompatible that a new perspective will emerge. If the same situation reoccurs frequently enough, the new perspective "will probably become an established part of a person's way of dealing with the world" (Becker et al. 1992: 35). The first year of medical school offers a good example of the genesis of new perspectives (the authors emphasize the fact that the situation is so "problematic" that students' perspectives reflect the pressure of their immediate academic context far more than prior roles and experiences), and also allows the influence of previous products of socialization to be identified (in order to explain the fraternity men's provisional perspective).

2.3 Two different conceptions of socialization

Comparing these two studies, with the same starting point, thus reveals different conceptions of socialization. If we were to retain just one of the polarizing contrasts between functionalism and interactionism in this regard, it would have to be the difference in sociological viewpoint: in the first case, we have an *ex post* viewpoint analyzing socialization in terms of its end and some of its products; in the second, we have a synchronous viewpoint observing socialization in action. Perhaps we do not need to choose between the two so much as we need to understand how they construct different subjects of study, whatever the type of socialization envisaged. Gender socialization, for example, can be studied *either* by looking retrospectively at how gender stereotypes are imposed and internalized in different social contexts, *or* by comparing learning processes among groups of boys and girls as they take place, looking also at those that are shared and those that are inverted. Another example would be analyzing school socialization *either* by focusing on the academic content of learning processes and how they establish the differentiated legitimacy of cultural products and family socialization, *or* by considering it as a process, observed in the day-to-day, during which, as noted earlier, students also learn things such as how to cheat, smoke at school, or think about other things while pretending to listen.

However, presenting these two approaches as entirely different from the point of view of socialization, with no common ground, is perhaps a pedagogical oversimplification that does not quite do justice to the analyses in question. The functionalist approach does take into account peer groups, interactions, and discontinuities in internalization, and the interactionist emphasis on the actor's own role in socialization does not erase the various institutional or interactional impositions that mean we cannot choose what we learn or what we become.

These two analytical lenses also have in common their focus on medical school: they therefore both necessarily leave to one side everything that happens afterwards, in which professional socialization is continued and extended. In this way, it is not limited to the students' years of explicit training and results in far more diversified effects than when they are put through a single "mold." Paradoxically, we still know very little about doctors' professional socialization over the life course, despite the importance of this particular case study for analyses of professional socialization in general. One recent article testifying to the "resurgence of medical education in sociology" raises the question of "socialization across the career path" and of the "institutions implicated in medical education" across the life course (for example, "medical board licensing examinations and continuing medical education requirements"), pointing to these as some of the "future directions where more research is needed" (Jenkins et al. 2021). It is also likely that, when it comes to the formative strength of practice, various influences operate together: the institutions where doctors practice medicine (with their different ideologies and working conditions); the peer group and other professional groups in different positions in the hospital hierarchy; membership in professional or political organizations or unions; life partners, friends, and so on.

Perhaps, at this point, we should therefore deduce that professional socialization is just as "plural" as primary socialization. This multiplicity is the focus of the following section.

3. Diverse secondary socialization

By focusing in detail on these two approaches to medical professional socialization, I chose to examine an important archetype in the history of sociology. The downside of this choice is that it inevitably provides only a partial vision of both professional socialization and secondary socialization. It is therefore necessary also to consider the broader space of secondary socialization, which obviously cannot be limited to the making of doctors nor, more generally, to professional socialization.

3.1 Other forms of professional socialization

The example of the "making of a physician" necessarily overemphasizes the importance of academic-professional learning and focuses on socialization to a very particular type of high-status profession.

Within the medical world itself, socialization processes are not the same among nurses as among doctors. While Hughes's passing through the mirror, described earlier, can theoretically be used to describe the "doctrinal conversion" (i.e. the shift from lay to professional conceptions) that takes place in the professional socialization of student nurses, this process involves content that is specific to their situation. As Fred Davis has shown, student nurses go through different stages in their doctrinal conversion: Initial Innocence (entailing feelings of disappointment and inadequacy); Labeled Recognition of Incongruity (experiencing the misalignment between their expectations and the actual curriculum); "Psyching Out" (divining what instructors expect of them); Role Simulation (the "performance implementation" of "psyching out"); Provisional Internalization (employing professional rhetoric, developing positive and negative reference models); and Stable Internalization (adopting an "assured stance towards their nursing performance," feeling "an ease at articulating the kind of nursing practice they believe in," and reinterpreting retrospectively their previous doubts). Insofar as this doctrinal conversion is relative to the institutional context in which it is fashioned, these transformations then continue in the next phases of the nurses' careers (Davis 1968).

Similarly, within "the professions," physicians' socialization processes are not the same as those of lawyers, for example, to cite another case traditionally examined in studies on professional socialization. As well as learning certain "skills and thinking styles" (Schleef 2006: 201), lawyers' professional socialization includes learning to internalize "ideologies about achievement and meritocracy" (4), as well as a – potentially critical and resistant – relationship to that ideology, resistance being "a vital component of the internalization of elite professional ideologies" (4).

Moreover, any "ordinary" salaried work is also likely to involve processes of professional socialization, even when these are not embedded in an educational setting or are not as institutionalized as those involved in the making of a doctor, hence the somewhat heterogeneous examples of professional socialization that have been studied. In addition to the traditional research on the professional socialization of teachers, clergy, nurses, social workers, and lawyers, studies have looked at the professional socialization of funeral directors (Cahill 1999), butchers, athletes, actors, prison wardens, sound engineers, strippers (women and men), police officers, professional card players, and accountants (Dubar 2004: 143). To give yet another example, the training of house prostitutes can also be defined as "a process of professional socialization" in which "the teaching Madam" employs a variety of techniques to train "turn-outs" in "sexual techniques" and "hustling skills" and to expose them to a set of occupational rules and values (Heyl 1977). Similarly, soccer players undergo professional socialization to their job, characterized by intensive training and a process through which they are progressively absorbed by a soccer "bubble" experienced as both a vocation and a passion, with a very uncertain relationship to the future (Bertrand 2011). Even sociology PhD candidates experience professional socialization (Li and Seale 2008), which, in some respects, resembles the socialization processes already cited, although it is closer to the experiences of medical students and soccer players than those of strippers or poker players. Even more glamorous than the experience of sociology PhD students, if that were imaginable, it is also possible to uncover how a person becomes a wildland firefighter (Desmond 2006), a boxer (Wacquant 2003), or a fashion model (Mears 2011) in the work of three sociologists who went through those processes.

There is clearly an element of "social bias" that results in studies on "professional socialization" focusing mainly on training modes that correspond to both the "school form" and high-status occupations. There is also a "methodological" bias that makes it harder to take a sociological approach to professional socialization when it does not occur through such an "educational" model. Explicit modes of training are often much easier to analyze. However, studying informal socialization is all the more interesting because it is not as easy to pinpoint as explicit professional training programs. This is particularly true for jobs that are considered low skilled and that enjoy little professional legitimacy. In these cases, social bias and methodological bias combine to render professional socialization and learning processes invisible. And yet there is, for example, such a thing as professional socialization to specialist assembly-line work, as outlined in Robert Linhart's

The Assembly Line (1981). The book recounts the experience of an activist intellectual working on an assembly line at the end of the 1960s, and its insights into how one learns both the job and the world of the factory are strengthened by the fact that the narrator was originally from a very different social sphere. In the case of state workers on front desks (in welfare offices, public services in working-class neighborhoods, and offices dealing with asylum seekers' applications) professional socialization is all relatively informal but no less present. Learning "what cannot be taught" is something that happens principally on the job, either in practice or by following the example of colleagues, thus reinforcing the importance of social judgments in these diffuse forms of socialization (Dubois 2010: 82–91). Similarly, the set of embodied habits and durable dispositions that make up the "bureaucratic habitus" of street-level bureaucrats working in Consulates is incorporated during a partly informal socialization process that takes place through contact with colleagues. It revolves around a "culture of suspicion" towards applicants, serving as a "sign of professionalism" and allowing "consular agents to deal with high numbers of applications under intense time pressure" (Alpes and Spire 2014: 269). In all of these jobs and professions, whether through explicit education, reference models, norms, or sanctions, but also, more discreetly, through repeated practices and interactions with colleagues, individuals incorporate habits, ways of seeing or doing things, and tendencies that are more than just skills or resources. Thus acquired, these habits, tastes, distastes, and inclinations transform individuals and make them do their work in a particular way.

3.2 Other forms of secondary socialization

As previously noted regarding *The Social Construction of Reality*, sociologists often equate secondary and professional socialization, whether implicitly or explicitly. And yet the former cannot be reduced to the latter. Just as we widened our focus from primary socialization in the original family unit to other agents of primary socialization and then to professional training, arguing that people and institutions other than the family have the strength to shape individuals, is it not also necessary to take into account the fact that contexts other than work have the power to reconstruct individuals after their primary socialization?

3.2.1 Marital socialization

Peter Berger, one of the authors of *The Social Construction of Reality*, answered this question in the affirmative. In an article co-authored with Hansfried Kellner in 1964, he suggested considering marriage (the institution, but above all the individual effects of married life) as a decisive socialization phase. According to the authors, the couple's life together – and particularly the "ongoing conversation" to which it gives rise, in which frameworks for defining reality inherited from prior socialization are confronted and exchanged – results in the internalization of a shared *nomos*, that is to say a shared frame of reference and action. This is illustrated, for example, in the way one of the partner's friendships may ultimately be "liquidated" after the marriage, as a result not of a deliberate decision by the one nor of deliberate sabotage by the other, but simply as a result of a marital socialization process that invisibly redefines relationships to the world and determines which friends are "good" or "bad." In terms of its strength, the process resembles primary socialization, but its structure is different. First, individuals play a more active role and contribute to defining the content of the socialization. However, whereas children are aware they are being formed by their parents and can feel this happening, the two partners are much less aware that marital socialization is taking place. They have the impression that their joint life has allowed them to "discover" "who they really are" and to realize "how they really feel and always have felt," but everything that they perceive as self-discovery (new tastes, practices, friends, and so on) is in fact an "invention," something they are co-constructing in their new life: rather than having each discovered themselves, they have in fact transformed one another (Berger and Kellner 1964). Various studies have shown the effects of marital socialization, for example regarding cultural practices (where one partner, especially when culturally dominant in relation to the other, may act as a powerful agent of cultural socialization [Lahire

2004]) or regarding political participation (the degree of partners' political participation tends to align after marriage [Stoker and Jennings 1995: 421]). However, Streib's research on cross-class marriages (2015), cited in Chapter 1, has shown that despite married life sometimes representing a far longer period than the time spent in families of origin, the transformation of one partner's class dispositions is by no means automatic, and even when limited transformations do occur, or when common ground is negotiated, the weight of the past continues to structure both partners' sensibilities (for example, regarding money or parenting). Emotions constitute an exception in this regard: "compared to any other sensibility, respondents more often felt that their own emotional sensibilities changed" (Streib 2015: 180). For this reason, research into emotional socialization is particularly interesting and we shall return to this in the next chapter.

Analyses of people's private lives seeking to track processes that are equivalent to "learning a job" have also looked at contexts beyond marital socialization. To cite another salient example, parental socialization also exists, refashioning individuals to make them into "parents" and doing so very differently according to gender. "A father's job" and "a mother's job" (with the latter in fact beginning with "the job of being pregnant") are learned through a plural socialization process emanating from a range of agents in the family, medical, professional, media, and scientific spheres. This is evidenced by the fact that almost all the agents of childhood socialization outlined in Chapter 2 also function as agents of parental socialization: extended family, friends, those responsible for childcare, experts and childhood professionals, but also school, which can be seen as the locus for a socially variable process through which individuals learn how to do their jobs as parents. Life, which could be described as made up of different jobs, therefore entails different forms of secondary socialization.

3.2.2 Group socialization
Among these different forms, the final one we shall look at here is the socialization that takes place within more or less institutionalized groups of individuals outside the context of family or work.

In this respect, it is important to recall the importance of spatial dimensions, which play a considerable role in the institutionalization of groups, that is to say in both the effectiveness and legitimacy of the socializing interactions that take place within them. A person's "neighborhood" or place of residence, for example, is the locus for secondary as well as primary socialization. As Japonica Brown-Saracino's study *Novel LBQ Identities in Four Small Cities* shows, "places make us" and transform us in ways that are city specific. For example, in the case of Sam, who moved from Boston to Portland and went from being a "lesbian" – in her own eyes and practices – to being a "stone butch"; or Lisa who, when she moved from Northampton (MA) to Ithaca (NY), was surprised (and regretted) that she did not think of herself or define herself as a lesbian as much as before. Each of the four cities studied by Brown-Saracino is the locus for a specific sexual identity culture that varies by city and governs the way in which her respondents "talk about or describe themselves, their coming out practices and even whether they prioritize being 'out' and 'proud', the degree to which they seek to build ties with heterosexuals, and their attitudes about contemporary LGBTQI politics and issues, such as marriage equality and transgender rights." The way in which places shape how we think about ourselves and interact with others is not limited to the LBQ individuals who were the focus of the study. According to Brown-Saracino, "to varying degrees, places make all of us" and "the way one 'does' professor, doctor, plumber, or stay-at-home-mom is different in Santa Fe than in Denver," just as "what it feels like to be single or married varies between Tampa and Tallahassee." Similarly, an adolescent "navigating the sometimes rocky transition from childhood to adulthood" might become "one teenager in Syracuse and another in Albany" (Brown-Saracino 2018: 5–6, 238). There remains much research to conduct and many processes to uncover regarding how we are constructed by places and perhaps particularly *what* exactly it is in places that constructs us: walls, how space is organized, and material living conditions, as we saw in Chapter 1, but also the institutions located in a place, its inhabitants and their social characteristics, and the way these inhabitants themselves incorporate and embody a specific, local identity culture that they transmit through interactions, as suggested by Brown-Saracino.

In an altogether different setting, group religious socialization occurs in Evangelical communities when members are socialized to the normative frame of sincerity, in particular to cultural understandings of how prayer should be performed and experienced (Winchester and Guhin 2019). Even a group with low levels of formal organization can be an agent of socialization, as shown by Howard Becker's famous analysis of marijuana smokers. He describes the group of smokers as the main medium through which an individual acquires the technique for smoking and learns to perceive and enjoy the effects. This learning process does not take place independently of the group. On the contrary, it is the deviant group that takes the marijuana smoker from one phase of the "career" to the next (Becker 1963: 41–58). Similarly, Alfred Lindesmith's study on opium addiction, often cited by Becker, shows how the group functions as a "socializing mechanism" in progressive drug dependency, providing individuals with an interpretive framework for their sensations, in particular equating the identification of withdrawal symptoms with the need for another fix (Becker 1970: 298).

This issue intersects with the broader question of the influence of "networks" on individual choices, which Paul DiMaggio and Filiz Garip (2012) have shown affects the reproduction of social inequalities in areas as varied as technology, labor markets, education, demography, and health. As for more institutionalized groups, a substantial amount of research into this kind of socialization can be found in the analyses of political sociology.

3.2.3 Political socialization

For a long time, political sociology focused solely on the family transmission of explicitly political values (during primary socialization), before moving beyond this dual limitation and examining secondary socialization and its practical and dispositional effects within but also outside the political sphere itself (Bargel and Darmon 2017). However, as a book written in the 1980s argued, attention to political socialization over the entire life span is still the exception rather than the rule (Sigel 1989), and this remains true today.

Yet analyzing adult political socialization can prove especially fruitful and this form of socialization can have very profound effects on people, beyond the sphere of politics per se, as demonstrated in a study by Javier Auyero and Claudio Benzecry on "socialization to a clientelist habitus" examining the "practical and dispositional" consequences of "clientelist politics." Daily participation in the world of grassroots politics "socializes agents into arbitrary (i.e. particular to a specific social group) ways of understanding political work" and leads them progressively and unconsciously to incorporate dispositions and a clientelist habitus that guides "their behavior and thoughts" in such a way that it "permeates all spheres of everyday access to resources (food, water, housing, cash transfer programs, school supplies)." Rather than simply being a political disposition, only activated in elections, this is therefore a more systematic clientelist habitus (Auyero and Benzecry 2017).

Among the various agents of adult political socialization that can be analyzed, activist socialization (i.e. the effects that participating in associations, trade unions, or political parties has upon activists) yields particularly useful insights. Studies have shown, for example, how in some cases activist socialization is also a form of largely informal professional socialization to a career in politics (Bargel and Darmon 2017). More generally, such analyses can also reveal "the organizational moulding of activism" (Sawicki and Siméant 2010) and show how participating in movements (through the repetitive practices involved and commitment to the group and its activities) is likely to constitute a powerful agent of socialization. Oliver Fillieule identifies three dimensions to this: "the acquisition of 'know-how' and 'wisdom' (resources); a vision of the world (ideology); and the restructuring of sociability networks in relation to the construction of individual and collective identities (social networks and identities)" (Fillieule 2010: 7).

Finally, political engagement can also have sociobiographical effects on a much broader scale, across a whole life course. As Fillieule has summarized, the biographical consequences of participating in social movements have been identified in "research on 1960s American activists," "studies of black student activists in the civil rights and black power movements and of riot participants," and work examining "the development of gender consciousness through the women's movement" (2013: 3–4). As Fillieule and his co-author Erik Neveu state, in an edited volume devoted to the long-term impact of activism, "political commitment generates or modifies dispositions to act, think, and perceive" (in the political but also extra-political spheres, at work or in family life) "in a way that is either consistent with or in contrast to the results of previous socialization" (2019: 3). Secondary political socialization therefore also raises the question of its interconnections with the effects of prior socialization, making it necessary to consider the links between at least two different moments of socialization. This means looking at (1) how the dispositions and skills internalized by individuals during earlier socialization processes lead them to being involved in activism, and (2) how that involvement itself produces processes of activist socialization that transform these dispositions – or even dispositions in other areas, as in the example of socialization to a clientelist habitus. A similar example can be seen in the case of African participants at the World Social Forum, who are predisposed to activism and internalization by their prior family, school, and religious socialization, and whose practices and representations of self are then in turn transformed by this internationalization and by their membership of an NGO (Siméant 2013).

To conclude, and looking back at what we have learned in this chapter, the focus on the "making of physicians" offered insight into the details of one particular type of secondary socialization but also showed how diverse the processes covered by that expression are: secondary socialization is clearly just as multi-faceted as primary socialization. First, it is diverse because it can take place within a range of different institutions: professional training establishments, employment settings, couples, peer groups, political parties, trade unions, political or religious organizations (and this list is by no means exhaustive). Second, it is also plural because, whether they cohere or compete, these different agents of socialization can act upon the individual at the same time, thus raising the same problems as those mentioned in Chapter 2 regarding the relationship between different, synchronous types of socialization. Finally, the question of these interconnections also emerges diachronically with these forms of "secondary" socialization that act upon an "already constituted self." While this takes us back to the starting point of this chapter, we still have a little way to go before the question can be addressed fully. Rather than juxtaposing an initial stage in which individuals are created and a second stage when they are re-created, it is worth examining the relationship between the products of successive socialization processes (and particularly the question of whether they are transformative or not) by taking a more continuous view of socialization – a perspective I shall now adopt in the next chapter.

4
Studying People-Building: Socialization across the Life Course

One common sociological view of how primary and secondary socialization fit together frames the process as discontinuous, with periods during which individuals are shaped or reshaped by society, followed by other periods during which they themselves act and, in doing so, actualize their prior socialization. Taken to the extreme, it is possible to imagine an anthropological cycle of forms of socialization common to all individuals across different societies: primary socialization in childhood and adolescence, followed by an initial short period of actualization, and then, with entry into adult life, a second wave of different forms of secondary socialization followed by a much longer, perhaps even definitive, period of actualization.

However, while overall this order of things is probably valid for the structure of most modern forms of socialization, it is doubtful that drawing a strict distinction between moments of socialization and moments of actualization is relevant except in purely analytical terms. Given the diverse socializing agents and mechanisms involved, given the varying and socially determined timeframes over which they operate, and given, finally, society's undeniably powerful capacity to shape us, it seems far more realistic to assume that society acts *continuously* upon individuals over the life course.

The notion of "continuous socialization" is sometimes put forward as a remedy against conceptions of socialization that are viewed as "too deterministic," because it seems to offer a way of diluting the effects of agents of socialization over a long time period, leaving more room for allegedly independent individual action. This is not the point of view I defend in this chapter, which takes the opposite theoretical stance. Just as Chapter 2 showed that the multiplicity of socialization did not make it weaker but rather revealed its power, so this chapter demonstrates the intensity of socialization even when it is potentially continuous. Is it not in fact logical that the longer socializing action lasts, the more determining it will prove?

This "logic," however, quickly comes up against what seems to be a paradox: how can socialization be both continuous and powerful, in other words, how can it have both formative and transformative effects on an individual? If the mark that society makes upon us is so strong that we are powerfully and definitively modeled "from the outside," then surely primary socialization, and family socialization in particular, constructs individuals who do nothing more than actualize the effects of this socialization throughout their life, in their actions, attitudes, and tastes? And is it not then sociologically inconceivable for those individuals to be transformed later? Conversely, if socialization is a continuous process, if an individual is incessantly reconstructed and transformed throughout the life course, then is it not necessarily without lasting effects? Devising a model in which socialization can be conceived of as a process that is both strong *and* continuous is one of the main issues addressed by the present chapter. I propose an analytical framework that can serve as a guide for taking a sociological approach to continuous socialization by considering it from three complementary points of view: the agents through which it operates, the way in which they function, and the effects they have upon individuals.

1. The agents of continuous socialization

In the first chapters of this book, we encountered a range of agents, both collective entities and individual actors, liable to shape the individual through their actions: parents, the rest of the family, childcare and childhood professionals, the media and cultural industries, the peer group, school, the professional world, spouses, and groups of various kinds. Moreover, we saw that they could operate via individual people, oral or written norms, material conditions of existence, or prescribed uses of spaces or objects. This chapter takes a more general perspective, considering these agents in terms of their sociological nature. It focuses, first, on an evident type of agent of socialization (frequently discussed in these pages, but not yet as a topic in its own right), namely institutions, and, second, on two further agents that seem, at first glance, very far from the institutional model of socialization, namely events and individual "will."

1.1 The central role of institutions and their limitations

Institutions – that is to say all "legitimized social grouping[s]," to take up Mary Douglas's definition (1986: 46) – are probably the most obvious agents of socialization: in order to form and transform an individual, institutional force seems indispensable, as the examples of family and school in particular seem to illustrate. However, we do not only encounter institutions in our early years and institutions are therefore essential foundations for continuous socialization.

1.1.1 Total institutions

Certain institutions constitute classic examples of what Michel Foucault referred to as an "apparatus for transforming individuals" (1995: 233), in relation to "disciplinary institutions" such as convents, schools, factories, hospitals, prisons, or the army: "by the eighteenth-century, the soldier has become something that can be made; out of a formless clay, an inapt body, the machine required can be constructed" (135). Foucault shows, more specifically, that these institutions "correct," "train," and "produce" individuals through "hierarchical observation," "normalizing judgement," and "their combination" in the procedure of "the examination" (135–94, 233). Similarly, the "total social institutions" grouped together by Erving Goffman (homes for various categories of individuals, hospitals, prisons, monasteries, and convents, but also army barracks, ships, and boarding schools) are each according to him "a natural experiment on what can be done to the self" (1961: 12). As a result of their common central feature – the fact that all aspects of life are embedded in the same institutional framework – they constitute an almost laboratory-like experiment in which the socializing influence of a given institution can be assessed (2–12). Studies focusing on psychiatric hospitals, such as the one by Goffman himself, but also, more generally, all those that focus on institutions that transform people, very clearly reveal the institutional force that is deployed to this end.

This theme gained prominence in the sociology of the 1960s and 1970s, notably in the United States. In his seminal article on the issue, Hasenfeld (1972) distinguishes between two types of related but distinct institutions: "people-processing institutions" and "people-changing institutions" (see also Darmon 2012). He defines the former as those "attempting to achieve changes in their clients not by altering basic personal attributes, but by conferring on them a public status" (1972: 256). Their activity thus mainly consists in managing flows of people whom they do not transform directly, but instead whose official definitions they change. Examples given in the article include a diagnostic clinic, a university admissions office, and a juvenile court. On the other hand, "people-changing institutions" directly alter people's behavior: they genuinely transform individuals themselves, not only managing them but making them. Typical examples of such institutions studied in the 1960s and 1970s include schools, mental hospitals, prisons, and correctional facilities.

But do such institutional modes of action still exist today? Could it not be said that our day and age is characterized instead by a decline in the socializing and transformative power of institutions? Are new institutional forms still transformative? Rather than trying to reach an overall historical verdict on the links between institutions and contemporary society, it is perhaps preferable to frame the limits of institutions' transformative power as an analytical question that can then be addressed empirically on a case-by-case basis.

1.1.2 A model for analyzing the socializing effects of institutions

Howard Becker proposed a model intended to allow for a more fine-grained, complex analysis of institutions' socializing effects (from any time period and of any nature) and to measure the limitations of their actions upon the individual (Becker 1970: 289–303). He suggested taking into account four "important discoveries" made by sociological studies focusing on adult socialization in institutions with an explicit mandate to transform "recruits" (schools, prisons, psychiatric hospitals). The first discovery in question is that the effects of this type of socialization cannot be equated either with the explicit aims promoted by the institution or with their polar opposites – something to which the interactionist approach to deviance is often reduced. Prison, for example, produces neither reformed individuals who have made a complete break with their criminal dispositions, nor more hardened, experienced criminals; instead, there is a far more complex career and the "curve of 'criminalization'" is not a "straight one slanting up." Second, Becker points to the danger inherent in thinking of "the institution" as a monolithic entity whose transformative forces all work in the same direction, underestimating divergences between groups or individual agents belonging to that institution. A classic theme in interactionist approaches to psychiatric hospitals, for example, consists in emphasizing the diverse "ideologies" represented within them. Third, Becker notes that the human "material" upon which the institution acts does not necessarily respond at the level of single individuals, but can do so as an organized group – the reader will recall *Boys in White*, discussed in the previous chapter, and the collective "student culture" resulting from the particular institutional socialization at work in medical school. Finally, Becker argues that it is imperative to take into account the determining influence of the "world beyond the socializing institution," in other words the social structures in which any institution is necessarily embedded – even when an institution is "total" and seemingly closed it is never an "empire within an empire," to borrow Spinoza's expression.

As Becker himself suggests, these analytical principles can also be used to study the socialization carried out by less institutionalized groups, or even the influences seemingly conveyed only by individuals. In all cases, however, from the socialization perspective that interests us here, it is important to introduce into Becker's model a further dimension that he tends to set aside but which is a frequent limitation placed upon institutional power: the way in which socializing influences encounter propensities within each individual that facilitate – or not – their transformation to different degrees. In this way, Goffman (1961: 12–13) suggests that the total institution can, to some extent, clash with individuals' "presenting culture" (i.e. the effects of their prior socialization) when they enter the institution.

Furthermore, based on the study of a Chicago gym training professional and amateur boxers, Loïc Wacquant has emphasized the existence of social conditions for success produced by this "little milieu" (2003: 127). These include:

> (self-)selection, which tends de facto to exclude the most excluded [and] operates not via the constraint of a penury of monetary means but through the *mediation of* [...] *moral and corporeal dispositions* [...] that are within reach of [only specific fractions] of the African-American population. [...] [T]o become a boxer requires a regularity of life, a sense of discipline, a physical and mental asceticism that cannot take root in social and economic conditions marked by chronic instability and temporal disorganization. (Wacquant 2003: 43–4)

Boxers are not recruited from "among the most disenfranchised fractions of the ghetto subproletariat" but rather from "those segments of its working class that are struggling at the threshold of stable socioeconomic integration." The effectiveness of institutional action therefore relies on the preconditioning provided by the working-class habitus and the way it suits the rigorous demands of boxing:

> One of the reasons why boxers are able to bear such wilful Spartanism is found in its affinity with their social conditions of origin: for most fighters, self-denial has been woven into the fabric of daily life since childhood. Boxing gives a more systematic, codified, and (for some) profitable expression to an all-too-familiar experience of deprivation rooted in racial and class exclusion. (Wacquant 1995: 81)

The gym therefore transforms bodies and individuals who are socially predisposed to being transformed in that way.

Similarly, to give another example, processes of organizational socialization alone cannot explain how a person becomes a wildland firefighter. These processes of organizational socialization "are specified extensions of earlier processes of socialization that take place during firefighters' childhood and adolescence" and "individual competences and dispositions acquired from a certain family and class background pre-condition rural working-class men for the rigors of firefighting" (Desmond 2006: 287).

Moreover, Lahire has shown that there are various social conditions of possibility, in the day-to-day, that determine the influence of peer groups or "secondary" significant others such as spouses. These socializing agents may, for example, represent more socially legitimate models or hold a moral, emotional, or religious authority that reinforces their prescriptive power. But it is also important to consider that an individual can either have or not have (sometimes latent) dispositions that are congruent with such influences from friends or partners (Lahire 2004: 471–96). The socializing power of different agents of socialization must therefore be analyzed not only in terms of the characteristics of the agents in question, but also in terms of the "human material" on which they work.

Finally, there are cases in which contradictions exist between the dispositions resulting from previous socialization processes and the context, field, or social space. Auyero and Benzecry explain that

> for Bourdieu, one of the causes of dispositional transformation is when the conditions of operation of the habitus are incongruent with the conditions of its acquisition, and thus causing change or transformation as they become "denaturalized," suggesting then that a transformed environment should also result in an eventual transformation of its representation. (2017: 193)

However, the authors' study of the clientelist habitus shows that, in that case, on the contrary, individuals engage in active work "to make sure the world still operates under the logic of practice they know and go by." As a result, the discrepancies between their dispositions and the conditions of operation can result in "social continuity instead of social change" (193). Whether individuals' predispositions help or hinder a given transformation, they must be taken into account if we want to understand whether an institution or any other agent of socialization has a transformative effect.

1.2 Processes beyond socialization?

If institutions are ideal-typical agents of socialization, it is probably because they possess something that appears to be a *sine qua non* condition for transforming individuals: they are able to control and oversee people's lives for the length of time necessary to instill dispositions. Does this mean, however, that socialization cannot take place outside such an apparatus, over a shorter timeframe or when an individual is alone? Events and personal will are often presented as stumbling blocks for, or exceptions to, socialization and yet they can both in fact operate as agents of socialization.

1.2.1 Events

The unpredictable, novel, and one-off nature of events seems to allow them to act upon individuals in a very different way than socializing agents, and this could give the impression that they escape the influence of socialization. Yet the sociology of continuous socialization can in fact encompass the effects of events in its model. In his approach to the "effervescence that is characteristic of revolutionary or creative epochs," Durkheim pointed out that a great collective upheaval can result in "man [...] becoming something other than what he was." The kind of transformations to which Durkheim was referring were limited in time, such as the one that occurred on the night of August 4 (in the French Revolution), when "an assembly was suddenly carried away in an act of sacrifice and abnegation [abolishing the privileges of the nobility] that each of its members had refused to make the night before and by which all were surprised the morning after" (1995: 212–13).

However, the effects of political events are not necessarily limited to a single night of effervescence and they can transform individuals in lasting ways. In his study of volunteers from the Freedom Summer of 1964, one of the key moments in the Civil Rights Movement in the United States, Douglas McAdam (1988) demonstrated that the lives of those who participated were shaped and transformed in ways that differed significantly when compared to people from similar social backgrounds who applied as volunteers but did not take part. The socialization processes that affected those who experienced the "freedom high" of this event produced a range of consequences. They became politically radicalized, felt marginal and out of place in the white, bourgeois society of the North, and began to link personal and political change through the political significance of personal lives. Similarly, studying the events of May 1968 in France, Julie Pagis has shown their role in processes of political socialization. She highlights their immediate socializing effects, according to people's degree of exposure and activist resources, but also their "long term consequences," demonstrating that, up to forty years later, they had a variable impact – depending on each person's social situation – in the political sphere (activism), the professional sphere (determining career trajectories), and the private sphere (for example, their everyday life, their "vision of the couple," or their way of interpreting the world) (Pagis 2018: 81–116, 117–34).

The continuous socialization model can even be applied to events that do not seem to be collective in the same way as political events. Anselm Strauss proposed a typology of "transformations of identity" throughout the life course that includes both the "regulated status passages" that occur within institutionalized social hierarchies and the "turning points" constituted by personal events that force "a person to recognize 'I am not the same as I was, as I used to be'" (a student nurse who watches a patient die in her arms, a person who experiences or commits a betrayal, a musician who "goes commercial 'just for a while'" to earn some money) (Strauss 1977: 91–100). The predisposition to be transformed by a given event can once again be taken into account in these cases when evaluating the event's transformative power.

1.2.2 Individual effort
Just like events, individual effort and will are often viewed as a mode of transformation that lies beyond socialization.

Seen from this perspective, in self-transformation individuals throw off the shackles placed on them by society and socialize themselves, as it were. However, it can be argued that even when something seems to be purely the effect of personal will, it is always useful to look to how social and socializing influences are operating. This is precisely the role of sociology, which is the only scientific discipline that both addresses these sorts of questions and seeks to identify the influence of society and socialization in behavior that would otherwise appear to be the result of free will.

A study of the processes through which young girls become anorexic offers an extreme case of individual transformation that appears to be deliberate and that could, at first glance, seem to involve the "invention" of an anorexic self beyond any social constraints (Darmon 2017). The anorexic work of self-transformation is applied to physical appearance – through dieting, sports, and clothing – but also to somatic sensations and sometimes school work and cultural knowledge. The extreme discipline and meticulous regulation of their lives involved in the girls' work on the self are reminiscent of the actions of total institutions and also show that "will" can become a veritable agent of socialization in its own right. However, the "socializing will" is autonomous in appearance only and is itself a "socialized will": society plays a considerable role in this work on the self, even when it is taken to the extreme. In the case of young girls with anorexia, three intersecting socializing influences can be identified: (1) the local dynamic of interactions, and particularly the injunction to be thin that is prevalent among the peer group, family (mothers, sisters), and female friends; (2) the internal dynamic of dispositions inherited from prior socialization, themselves marked by four intersecting variables (era, social class, gender, and age) that each reinforce an ascetic relationship to the body making physical transformation a valued and realistic aim; and (3) the external dynamic of institutions and particularly the medical institution that can play a socializing role long before the hospital phase in the anorexic career.

It is therefore always worth engaging in empirical investigation to identify socializing influences, even in transformative processes that seem to take place independently, and it certainly seems that in fact neither events nor what appears to be individual effort place any limitations on the socialization model. It is possible to show not only that the effects of events and individual efforts depend on socialization processes but also that they themselves constitute agents of socialization in their own right, thus demonstrating that continuous socialization must not simply be reduced to the canonical model of the institution.

2. How continuous socialization functions

The question of how all these different agents of socialization operate is both fundamental and at the same time relatively absent from sociological research, no doubt because it seems to lie beyond the scope of sociology and to fall instead within that of either developmental psychology or cognitive science. In this regard, cognitive sociology is a promising developing field and if it focuses more closely and more empirically on the social processes of socialization, their variations, and the sociogenesis of dispositions, it will no doubt soon deliver important insights. In the meantime, within sociology more generally, specific approaches for analyzing how agents of socialization operate do in fact exist, which, without claiming to provide a general theory of mechanisms of internalization, can nevertheless illuminate certain aspects of the latter.

2.1 Diverse modes and mechanisms

It is perhaps the diverse range of modes in which socialization processes operate that is most striking. We have already seen, albeit sometimes implicitly, some of the analytical axes along which these can be positioned. For example, from the "education/socialization" opposition discussed in Chapter 1, we can infer a "degree of awareness" axis present during socialization, from the point of view of both those doing the socializing and those being socialized. While the specific position of given processes on this axis must be established on a case-by-case basis, we have also seen that structural hypotheses can be formulated in this regard. For example, as we have seen, it has been suggested that individuals being socialized are less aware of this during marital socialization than during childhood socialization (Berger and Kellner 1964), or that, again from the point of view of those being socialized, professional training and socialization are more reflexive and conscious than marital or childhood socialization.

A second axis on which some of the examples I have mentioned can be positioned is that of the apparent degree of constraint or violence: socialization processes can operate in "soft" and "hard" ways. As far as "hard" ways are concerned, we saw earlier the role of discipline and punishment in the institutions described by Foucault; as for softer forms, socialization by friends or partners is a good example of how the people closest to us and with whom we share moments, or even our lives, can "rub off" on us without our even being aware of it.

Finally, a typology drawn up by Lahire provides another axis of analysis, this time relating to the sociological nature of the mechanisms that form dispositions. Socialization can take place through direct training or action, by participating in recurring activities in the family, at school, among peers, or at work. But it can also be the result of a more diffuse effect of how a "situation" is organized (for example, the many apparatuses that separate the sexes, such as public toilets or locker rooms, which contribute "silently" to gender socialization). Socialization can, finally, proceed by the dissemination and inculcation of cultural norms, values, or models, that is to say injunctions concerning how one should see or express the world, whether these are transmitted by families, schools, or the cultural industries (Lahire 2002: 420–2).

2.2 Through body, speech, or writing?

The "silent socialization" just mentioned points to the key issue of the role of language in how socialization operates. I referred earlier, in the previous chapter, to the considerable importance given by Berger and Kellner to conversation in marital socialization. More generally, language is defined in *The Social Construction of Reality* as "the most important content and the most important instrument of socialization"

(Berger and Luckmann 1991: 153). From this perspective, if language possesses such power, it is because internalizing the categories it conveys means internalizing a whole world. When we encourage a child to "act like a brave little boy" (155), we are reproducing and constructing a world in which there are boys and girls, little children and grown-ups, those who are brave and those who are not (161–2).

Running counter to the notion that language is central, other conceptions emphasize the silence of bodies during internalization. In his participant observation study of becoming a boxer, Wacquant analyzes the principally corporeal, and correlatively very silent, "implicit, practical, and collective mode" (2003: 99) in which a boxer's habitus is instilled. The trainer only intervenes by means of very brief, diffuse instructions insofar as "the gist of pugilistic knowledge is transmitted outside of his explicit intervention, through a 'silent and practical communication, from body to body'" (113). This pedagogy, giving very little room to speech, draws in particular on the profoundly collective nature of the learning process, in which "pugilistic knowledge is [...] transmitted by mimeticism or countermimeticism," with each individual observing the others' gestures, or by the mutual (still tacit) correction that the group of boxers exercise over one another (117).

This approach has, however, received some criticism. Taking up Wacquant's material on the pugilistic learning process, Lahire highlighted a linguistic (albeit not necessarily intentional, reflexive, or intellectual) dimension that, in his view, Wacquant passed over in his analysis (2011: 163–74). Similarly, Wilfried Lignier has emphasized that "words also make us, which is to say that conceiving of socialization within the frame of the theory of practice is compatible with the idea that we are not only socialized through our body, but also through (practical) language" (2020: 18). For example, his ethnographical study, conducted with two- to three-year-old children in a French daycare center, shows how the caregivers' socializing injunctions are part of a particular ideology of childhood in which "caring for young children mostly consists of being aware of their personal desires and needs (rather than imposing any sort of norms on them)" (26). And yet, following the repetition of these injunctions and given the importance of daycare centers as agents of socialization, the children learn and incorporate a particular relationship to the self and come to adopt, when speaking of individual feelings, "the special view on violence, personal integrity, and social relationships" (27) that is encapsulated by these instructions: the children are in fact "made" by the words being used. Finally, in a recent study on the socialization to bodily comportment in two elementary schools, Peter Harvey shows that the transmission of embodied skills "requires the repetition of *both explicit and implicit lessons*" (2022: 1419).

It can therefore be argued that the way forward is to avoid underestimating either dimension, especially where we least expect to find them: for example, just as linguistic categories play a role in sporting socialization, so an important aspect of school socialization takes place "through the body." Finally, beyond the general debate about the role of language, it is also possible that not all forms of socialization involve the body and speech in the same proportions, and that this is yet another axis on which a given form of socialization can be situated, according to whether it is more or less linguistic or corporeal.

In constructing this axis, it could also be interesting to consider the role of the written word in socialization, which is less often addressed. What could be described as "the socializing written word" in fact has an important function in our societies and this is probably increasing thanks to digital texts. The written word (and the printed image) can function implicitly, by contributing to forming or transforming individuals' mental categories, for example when children's books continue to reproduce gender stereotypes (Williams et al. 1987) or to naturalize the division of labor and the embodied relations of class domination (Levi Martin 2000). Written socialization can also operate through direct injunctions and the explicit transformation of dispositions, for example in the case of the "panopticon on paper" governing bodies in a commercial weight-loss group (Darmon 2012). This example testifies more broadly to the role of written socialization in public health policy, revealing the importance of written instructions (today, in a digital format) typical of "information societies." It also shows how writing a diary can be used as a tool for control and highlights the role played by the mountain of written documents present in the members' homes, allowing the boundaries of the socializing institution to extend far beyond the brief interactions that take place between members and group leaders.

2.3 How processes of socialization "fit together"

Finally, analysis of how socialization processes work must necessarily include a dimension that is key to the continuous perspective: their temporal and sequential nature. I already mentioned, in Chapter 1, the many reasons that can explain the weight of primary socialization. These remain valid when considering socialization as continuous, while also maintaining that earlier experiences are more overdetermining than later ones because they close off future possibilities: what was experienced and internalized "before" becomes the basis for how what happens "after" is perceived and internalized. In Bourdieu's terms, one might say that "habitus helps to determine what transforms it" (2000: 149) or, in Berger and Luckmann's terms, that during a given socialization process (with the exception of very particular cases to which I shall return) "the present is interpreted so as to stand in a continuous relationship with the past" – the past of earlier socialization that constitutes the "reality-base" for the process in question (1991: 182)

The "continuous socialization" approach therefore considers how forms of socialization fit together rather than simply how they follow on from one another, or are juxtaposed, and it does so throughout the life course. In this regard, much work remains to be done on socialization processes in old age and at the end of life, looking, for example, at how one learns to become old in a particular way. These issues are widely understudied compared to the equivalent processes in childhood. In methodological terms, analyses of individual cases, retracing the life course of one or several people by gathering substantial amounts of information about each person and their history, are a particularly fruitful means through which to analyze how different forms of socialization fit together – something that is otherwise very difficult to access.

However, any investigation that pays attention to these interconnections between successive forms of socialization can identify them. Elizabeth Armstrong and Laura Hamilton's work on the trajectories of young women studying at a flagship Midwestern public university sheds light on how primary and secondary socialization fit together. Their research shows how the effects of institutional socialization – that is to say the way in which going to college transforms these girls – depends on who they were when they arrived, in other words on the dispositions they had acquired during their prior socialization. As individuals from "different social locations," the students started out with "different cultural tastes, knowledge about college, academic and professional skills, and social capacities" (Armstrong and Hamilton 2013: 263). They were either "primed to party," "cultivated for success," or "motivated for mobility." Their experiences were then "fundamentally shaped by the structure of academic and social life on campus" and its three different "pathways": the "party pathway" "provisioned to support the affluent and socially oriented," the "mobility pathway" "designed for the pragmatic and vocationally oriented," and the "professional pathway" suited to "ambitious students from privileged families" (15). Armstrong and Hamilton show that pathways "vary in the class resources necessary to have a positive experience during college and to translate that experience into a way of life beyond college" (216). For example, the party pathway "required the highest level of class resources to pursue without negative consequences," worked well for the young women who "had the time, money, and know-how to perfect gender- and class-specific interactional skills, appearances and cultural tastes," but "was a poor fit for anyone not advantaged in every possible way" (217).

Other studies, on the contrary, reveal contradictions between two particular moments and products of socialization processes within the same individual. For example, Kristen Schilt's work on transgender men in the workplace can be read in this light. Many trans men enter the workforce "as women" and then transition to adopt their male identity, which means they arrive with dispositions acquired during a socialization process that gendered them as women. Then, as men, they find themselves "receiving more authority, respect, and reward in the workplace than they received as women, even when they remain in the same jobs" (Schilt 2006: 265). The professional gender socialization at work operates differently than previous iterations of gender socialization. It can generate greater assurance, lead individuals to take more authority and space in the workplace, and produce a particular view of the working world and gender relations as a result of holding what Schilt describes as an "outsider-within" position. We can clearly see, in this example, that the process of professional socialization does not entirely overwrite the previous gender socialization, because the respondents

> maintain an internalized sense of being outsiders to the gender schemas that advantage men. This internalized insider/outsider position allows some transmen to see clearly the advantages associated with being men at work while still maintaining a critical view to how this advantage operates and is reproduced and how it disadvantages women. (Schilt 2006: 469)

The different processes of socialization that follow on from one another over the life course are not simply added together, they *fit* together. However, the possible ways in which this can happen depend on the order in which they occur (some types of primary/prior socialization will exclude the possibility of other types of secondary/later socialization for example) and also on social logics of path dependency (with prior socialization creating the dispositional conditions for the actions and types of influence of the socialization that then follows).

These questions therefore require greater attention to be paid not only to how different moments and types of socialization fit together, but also to the actual products of continuous socialization, which brings us to the topic of the third section of this chapter.

3. Continuous socialization: products and effects

Over the previous chapters, we have encountered highly diverse contents of socialization. It would not necessarily be heuristically useful to classify them according to whether they pertain to corporeal attitudes and habits or to mental values and representations: empirical reality undermines this distinction, showing that both aspects often prove to be intertwined. However, it is worth noting that the terms used to refer to the products of socialization tend to reflect the approach adopted, and specifically the contrast between Bourdieu's and Lahire's positions. On the one hand, emphasis is placed on the "systemic" nature of these products (systems of values, habitus, ethos, worldviews, worlds, and so on); on the other hand, their "contextual" and "autonomous" nature is underscored (dispositions to act, dispositions to believe, skills, corporeal attitudes, mental attitudes, opinions, beliefs, values, perceptive categories, perspectives, and so on). However coherent a whole these products may or may not form, approaching them from the perspective of continuous socialization means asking how they coexist, which brings us back to our initial paradox: can socialization be both continuous and powerful?

Before returning to this question, I shall take the same approach as I did earlier with agents of socialization, and consider these products by focusing first on those that might seem quite distant from, or even independent of, processes of socialization. I will then tackle the question of the transformation of individuals as a product of socialization, examining the extent to which successive socialization processes do or do not achieve this.

3.1 Emotions, feelings, and cognition: beyond socialization?

3.1.1 Continuous emotional socialization

The Durkheimian tradition, represented in this instance by Marcel Mauss, highlighted the deeply social nature of emotions and "the obligatory expression of feelings" that makes demonstrations of sadness or pain at a funeral "not exclusively psychological phenomena, or physiological, but social phenomena, eminently marked with the sign of non-spontaneity, and of the most perfect obligation" (Garces and Jones 2009: 298). Arlie Hochschild's work offers a way of pursuing this radical denaturalization of emotion (consisting in showing that "emotion is governed by social rules") and reinforcing it in three different ways, from the point of view of the sociology of socialization: (1) by introducing the notion of "emotion work," which shows how emotions are the result of an often unconscious learning process; (2) by envisaging different moments of emotion work over the life cycle, for example how it is learned in childhood and the different forms it takes in different professions; and (3) by re-embedding it within the social structure, in terms of class and gender.

First of all, emotions are something that we learn: we "feel gay at parties, sad at funerals, happy at weddings" because we have been "'socialized' to try to pay tribute to official definitions of situations, with no less than [our] feelings' (Hochschild 1979: 552). In other words, it is important to study the socialization of emotion from the very earliest age because "accumulating evidence suggests that socialization affects children's abilities to identify their own and others' emotional experiences and to control their own affective display" (Pollak and Thoits 1989: 22).

Primary class socialization can therefore explain the different ways in which adults have learned to "manage their feelings," preparing them – more or less well – to work in the "meaning-making jobs" that are more common among the middle classes and that place a higher premium on the individual's capacity to do emotion work. In the middle and upper classes, primary socialization focuses more on controlling emotions (children will be corrected or punished when they feel the wrong way, see things in the wrong light, or have the wrong intentions), whereas in the working classes the focus is rather on controlling behavior, in keeping with certain characteristics already identified in earlier chapters. For this reason, "working-class parents prepare the child to be controlled more by rules that apply to overt behavior whereas middle-class parents prepare them to be governed more by rules that apply to feelings" (Hochschild 2012: 156). As a result, "middle-class families prepare their children for emotion management more and working-class families prepare them less" (Hochschild 1979: 551), which means that these forms of primary socialization reproduce the class structure in emotional terms. Moreover, where gender in concerned, the emotional education of boys and girls differs in primary socialization, with a particular role imposed upon girls who learn to "do the work of affirming, enhancing, and celebrating the wellbeing and status of others" (Hochschild 2012: 165).

However, Hochschild's work also shows that emotions are far from only learned or worked upon in childhood or during primary socialization. Flight attendants and bill collectors, for example, have to provide emotional labor consisting in either prompting or repressing emotion with a view to maintaining the expected outer display that must in turn produce the appropriate state of mind in others. This specific labor is something that must be learned, with the example par excellence being the flight attendants' training centers in which Hochschild conducted her observations and first identified the presence of emotional labor in the advice "smile like you really mean it" (Hochschild 2012: ix). Flight attendants' emotional labor is a public and paid act; they are selected based on their capacity to provide it, they are trained for it, and they are supervised while doing it. With "the growth of large organizations calling for skills in personal relations, the womanly art of status enhancement and the emotion work that it requires has been made more public, more systematized, and more standardized" (171). This professional emotional socialization is even more gendered than primary emotional socialization and is congruent with prior gender and class socialization.

Learning emotion work and being socialized to emotion management are therefore central in certain types of professional socialization, especially those of middle-class women in jobs involving direct contact with the public. But more generally, and insofar as "there are jobs at every socio-economic level that place emotional burdens on the worker" (Hochschild 2012: 153), all professional socialization can include an emotional dimension and emotional socialization (in the sense of the emotional content of socialization, not the learning of emotion work) is continuous.

It can therefore be examined and investigated in the same way as other areas of continuous socialization, for example by looking at how it intersects with other forms of socialization. One study of this kind by Spencer E. Cahill showed how the occupational emotional socialization of mortuary science students is linked to their prior socialization (especially family socialization) that fostered a certain relationship to death. They see it as both routine and an object of curiosity – an attitude typically encountered among the children of funeral directors, who form a majority in this student body. Cahill suggests that

> over the course of their childhood socialization, individuals acquire (to draw [...] on Bourdieu) an emotional "habitus" or system of emotional dispositions. That system of dispositions, in Bourdieu's [...] words, is "general, transposable," and applied "beyond the limits of what has been directly learnt." That is, it generates emotional perceptions, reactions, expressions, and emotion management strategies across various situations, including those not encountered previously. (Cahill 1999: 112)

These emotional dispositions then go on to influence which occupations will seem desirable or not, and how later emotional socialization (professional, for example) will take place, depending on how much distance or difference there is between the dispositions resulting from primary socialization (the relationship to death among funeral directors' children) and the dispositions that their occupational socialization attempts to instill in them (the relationship to death and emotional management that their training in mortuary science leads them to incorporate) (Cahill 1999).

Once again, when examined through the lens of socialization, emotions are not a specific case: they have to be learned, working on them means managing them in ways that vary according to class and gender in primary socialization, and this is a continuous process that takes place across the life course and intersects with other areas of socialization as it does so.

3.1.2 Continuous sensorial and cognitive socialization
A second area in which the notions of socialization, incorporation, and learning may, at first glance, seem somewhat incongruous or irrelevant is that of cognition and sensoriality. However, as Eviatar Zerubavel, whose work I draw on

here, argues: "like any other social norm, cognitive norms are something that we learn. In other words, we learn how to focus our attention, frame our experience, generalize, and reason in a socially appropriate manner" (1997: 13). As we become socialized by this process of cognitive socialization "and learn to see the world as through the mental lenses of particular thought communities, we come to assign to objects the same meaning that they have for others around us, to both ignore and remember the same things that they do, and to laugh at the same things that they find funny" (15).

This cognitive and sensorial socialization is also a form of continuous socialization as we can see through the example of vision and optical socialization, which means we see certain things and disregard others. This is evidenced in the way children, "who have not learned yet how to focus their attention in a socially appropriate manner," "attend to that which is supposed to be disregarded." Zerubavel gives the example of a child who, "on his first visit to the zoo, instead of looking at the animals, kept focusing on the patterns in the chain-link fence" around them, while another, at the circus, could not "'see' the fine line that, to the adults around him, so clearly separates the elephant trainers 'in the spotlight' from the attendants who clean after them 'in the background.'" This shows us that "ignoring the irrelevant," or seeing fine lines, is "something we learn to do" (14) during a process of optical socialization that teaches us to consider some parts of reality as "mere background" (36).

This socialization is inseparably visual and cognitive. "Through the various norms of focusing we internalize as part of our 'optical' socialization, society essentially controls which thoughts even 'cross' our minds" (51). And far from remaining limited to childhood, this continues indefinitely throughout the life course. We learn that "in order to find a book in a bookstore, we must attend to the first letters of its author's name while ignoring the color of its cover" (13); we "likewise learn to 'see' the fine lines separating liberals from conservatives or the edible from the inedible" (14) (the latter is a learning process that begins in childhood but continues later and can lead to certain objects moving from one category to another, for example flowers or insects). Professional socialization provides many significant instances of this type of socialization, from young sociologists who learn to acquire what is aptly referred to as a "sociological eye" through which they develop their "sociological imagination" (to borrow the titles of two famous works of sociology) to radiologists who learn to read x-rays – both types of professionals learn what to look at, whether it be the link between social class and success at school or a spot that is not an artifact on an x-ray image.

There are many other examples of sensorial socialization, for example olfaction: how do we incorporate the nondeclarative culture that means we automatically associate a smell with a given emotion, place, or group of people, and how do these forms of sensorial socialization vary according to class, race, and gender (Cerulo 2018)? Another example is the somatic sensation after eating a copious meal: how do members of the working classes come to experience such a meal as providing an agreeable feeling of being pleasantly replete, whereas for members of the upper classes, it produces an unpleasant sensation of heaviness and of being too full (Boltanski 1971)?

Even in these cases where the innate and its reflexes seem all-powerful, we are also dealing with socialization processes and their products – both of which are strong (since they determine what we see, smell, feel) and continuous (since they begin in childhood but seem to operate throughout the life course). This brings us back to our initial paradox once again: can socialization be both continuous and powerful?

3.2 Socialization as both continuous and powerful?

In *Reproduction*, Bourdieu and Passeron draw a contrast between "conversion" – the complete substitution of one habitus for another – and "confirmation" – the maintenance or reinforcement of prior socialization with later socialization (1990: 44–5). This constitutes a final axis along which socialization can be analyzed, with many intermediate positions existing between these two extremes.

3.2.1 Reinforcement socialization
Within the model of continuous socialization, a given socialization operation can be a powerful person-shaping process

without necessarily being transformative. Such processes that above all "fix" in place the primary habitus can be referred to as "reinforcement socialization."

Gender socialization offers many examples of reinforcement socialization. It could even be argued that, to a large extent, the strength of gender socialization and the hysteresis of its products are the result of the series of "fixing" processes composing it over the life course. This can be seen, for example, in the way that masculine socialization is reinforced by socializing agents such as family, school, university, the peer group, sports, or the army (Bertrand et al. 2015), and in the way professional socialization in a field such as engineering reproduces and thus perpetuates sex segregation by leading women to internalize lower levels of confidence about whether they will "fit in" with the professional culture of engineering, thus diverting them from this profession (Seron et al. 2015).

Cases of gender socialization that do not reinforce prior socialization are certainly less common. We saw one example earlier, with the trans men who were successively socialized as women and then as men, and a further atypical example of this kind is provided by a classic case in the history of sociology, studied by Harold Garfinkel – the case of "Agnes," who "was born a boy" (1967: 120) and who elected to change sex. Examined within the framework of the sociology of socialization, paying particular attention to learning processes, the incorporation of dispositions, and the timeframes of both, all the work Agnes does upon herself (practicing feminine postures in front of a mirror, sticking to a particular diet, and learning from her partner's mother how to cook and sew, and what constitutes good taste for a woman) can be seen as transformative socialization rather than reinforcement socialization.

There is no necessary link between certain institutions and reinforcement socialization, and there are not, on the one hand, institutions that reinforce, and on the other institutions that transform. As we have already seen, the socializing effect of an institution, or more broadly of an agent of socialization, is subject to variations that derive from the encounter between the institution in question and the internalized products of prior socialization. For example, school socialization – especially during the child's first years at school – can, as we saw in Chapter 2, be transformative for some, while for others it will reinforce existing "school" dispositions, depending on the extent to which school socialization is congruent with their prior family socialization: there is no *necessary* link between one type of institution and one type of socialization; rather there are specific processes and variations, to be uncovered in each case observed.

3.2.2 Conversion socialization

At the other end of the spectrum to these forms of reinforcement socialization are the processes referred to as "conversion socialization," that is to say processes that effect total and radical transformations, on the model of religious conversion. The topic seems to have fascinated a great many sociologists and I shall simply mention here a few of the numerous examples of this secularization – and sociologization – of the concept. Looking back, Durkheim gave such importance to it that it was his point of reference for defining education as a "slow" conversion:

> True conversion involves a profound movement as a result of which the soul in its entirety, by turning in a quite different direction, changes its position, its stance, and as a result modifies its whole outlook on the world. [...] [T]his same shift of perspective can come about slowly as a result of gradual and imperceptible pressure; this is what happens as a result of education. (1977: 29)

Bourdieu and Passeron use the Greek word *metanoia* to emphasize the radical nature of these transformations – the term means "conversion" and involves the idea of mutation and rebirth. In the context of a theory of habitus, particularly advanced "deculturating and reculturating techniques" are necessary in order "to produce a habitus as similar as possible to that produced in the earliest phase of life, while having to reckon with a pre-existing habitus" (Bourdieu and Passeron 1990: 39), or, in other words – those used in Chapter 1 – to replace "irreversible dispositions" with "other irreversible dispositions." The apparent contradiction in terms here reveals the paradoxical interest shown in conversion by sociologies that, like Durkheim's and Bourdieu's, also establish the strength of primary socialization and hysteresis, and that therefore have to contend with the question of whether conversion is even possible. The theme is also present in Berger and Luckmann's work, when they address what they refer to as "alternations": extreme cases "in which the individual 'switches worlds,'" that is to say in which a process of socialization occurs that effects a "total" transformation – or one that is quasi-total since, as they put it, "at the very least the transformed individual will have the same body and live in the same physical universe" (1991: 176).[5] Alternation therefore involves re-socialization processes that resemble those of primary socialization in their radical and probably affective nature; this re-socialization differs from primary socialization, however, insofar as it does not take place *ex nihilo* and must "dismantle" the products of prior socialization. Once again, Berger and Luckmann foreground the model of religious conversion and mention psychotherapy and political indoctrination (citing the "brainwashing" techniques in Communist China, an example often given by Cold-War-era American sociologists when discussing conversion processes).[6] They also highlight a particularly important dimension of conversions: the conditions necessary in order for them to produce their effects. They show that it is not the mystical crisis in itself that produces the convert, but rather the fact that the convert is then embedded in a social structure that "confirms" the products of this re-socialization day after day and allows the individual to *remain* converted. To turn Durkheim's formula on its head, one might say that "conversion is education" and thus also requires time and repeated practices in order to produce socialization effects. The radical nature of the transformation that results from alternations also requires substantial biographical work, which is the only exception to the rule identified by the authors according to which the past of prior socialization is the reality-base for the present. In the case of alternations, it is on the contrary the present of the radical transformation that becomes the sole filter through which individuals envisage the products of their prior socialization, reinterpreting their personal past to make it conform to the present reality (Berger and Luckmann 1991: 176–81).

Approaching processes of individual transformation via the notion of "conversion" also allows us to consider all the opposing processes and phenomena that occur during these conversions. The conversion model can account for both the hysteresis (i.e. the maintenance and resistance) and the reversibility (i.e. the potential transformation) of dispositions, just as it can address practical changes and actual transformations, as well as discourses and representations of self-transformation. Moreover, the notion allows various other factors to be examined: the processual characteristics of transformation work (which takes place over time and is not instantaneous, although it may sometimes appear that way); the social conditions of possibility for people to change (relating to their predisposition to be changed by a given process of transformation); and the way conversions are embedded in an oriented social space, structured in particular by class and gender (even when the transformations that affect individuals seem neutral or without any particular connotations, it is often productive to try to identify their social stakes and to bring out any unconscious or unnoticed positions or directions in the social space).[7]

3.2.3 Transformative socialization

Many sociological approaches have been used to study conversion processes, even though the latter are probably not particularly frequent in real life. As such, their analysis serves as an extreme case in the light of which less pronounced but more common situations of socialization can also be examined: all those that do not result in the total and radical transformation of the individual, but nevertheless do not simply confirm and reinforce past socialization. All these processes that transform the individual to some degree or other, on some level or other, can thus be described as "transformative socialization," which is by definition *limited* compared to what a conversion process would entail.

The effect of transformative socialization can, first, be limited in time. Goffman suggests that, despite the considerable reach of total institutions' power, the "rehabilitation" carried out within their walls does not have lasting effects on the inmates once they leave. He mentions in passing that some lasting changes can result from the institutional socialization they have experienced, but adds that these do not necessarily correspond to the stated aims of the institution itself (1961: 71).

The effects of transformative socialization can also be limited in terms of the areas to which they apply. Running counter to a model of school conversion according to which cases of academic success in working-class backgrounds can only be the result of a radical transformation of the child's whole person and "working-class" tastes or allegiances, Lahire reveals many cases in which the effects of school socialization are limited to a very circumscribed area of practice. This was the case, for example, for two young women from, respectively, lower-middle- and working-class backgrounds who obtained the *agrégation* in French literature (a prestigious competitive examination qualifying them to teach in secondary education): the women had extremely legitimate literary practices as a result of having acquired cultivated dispositions at school, but their sense of cultural legitimacy was limited to literature alone and extended to almost no other cultural domains whatsoever (Lahire 2004: 147–59).

Similarly, two studies on areas as different as commercial weight-loss groups and post-stroke rehabilitation facilities show that the implicit model directing the actions of these institutions is that of conversion. They count on the total and radical transformation of their working-class members: in the first case in terms of the dieters' eating habits, but also more generally their daily lives, sociability, domestic arrangements, etc.; in the second case in terms of the patients' relationship to impairment, to learning, to daily organization, to the written word, to improvisation and planning, etc. (Darmon 2012; 2020). Such conversions in fact prove impossible, especially because they presuppose certain relationships to the written word, to learning, or to the world that are those of the middle and upper classes with significant levels of cultural capital, rather than those of the working-class people the institutions generally deal with. Consequently, the transformations that are nevertheless effected by these institutions' processes of socialization remain limited to practices or areas that are compatible with the preexisting working-class dispositions of their members.

Given that reinforcement socialization exists, it is perfectly possible to be continuously socialized without being continuously transformed; similarly, given that transformative socialization exists, it is also possible to be transformed by a socialization process without being transformed completely or definitively. Socialization can therefore be strong and continuous without this signifying that total, radical transformations keep occurring one after another throughout the life course. Moreover, the continuous nature of society's action upon the individual does not necessarily erase the essential and over-determining nature of certain agents or moments in individuals' social construction, but rather repositions them within a longer and more varied process. The presence of this continuity and variety is why establishing a stark distinction between "primary" and "secondary" socialization is ultimately not as productive as it might first appear. It introduces a theoretical discontinuity that can be difficult to apply: does school, for example, fall under the remit of primary or secondary socialization? Should preschool be considered separately from university in this regard, or should we instead focus on the things they have in common? Should we draw a distinction between preschool as primary socialization for the children of preschool teachers and as secondary socialization for working-class children, given the greater distance between school norms and models and those present in the latter's family socialization? Moreover, any recourse to a strict distinction between primary and secondary socialization also presents the disadvantage of placing under the same label forms of socialization that can be very different and for which the descriptors "primary" and "secondary" are far from sufficient: for example, in the case of "secondary socialization," marital and professional socialization; or professional socialization that takes place over a whole stretch of the life cycle and very short institutional socialization, such as during a hospital stay. It can therefore be argued that more enriching, more precise, and more enlightening insights can be afforded by defining and distinguishing successive forms of socialization in different ways depending on the research approach adopted. They can be defined according to the social identity of the agent responsible for them (referring to family, school, peer, or professional socialization, for example) or according to the sociological nature of that agent (referring to institutional or group socialization, for example). They can also be defined according to how they function (referring to socialization through education, example, situation, language, practice, and so on) or according to the effects they have upon the individual (referring to reinforcement, conversion, or transformative socialization). This allows their position in the life course to be specified (e.g. childhood, adolescent, or adult socialization, socialization to old age), but also, and above all, their position within the series of different processes that make up continuous socialization.

Applying these various approaches to socialization across the life course is not without its challenges, however, and the next and final chapter will outline and address some of these, arguing that they in fact make the sociology of socialization more not less relevant to our understanding of contemporary society.

5
Engaging with Challenges Old and New: Race, Gender, Children's Agency

Drawing on the tools provided by the previous chapters, I shall now turn to some fundamental questions that have not yet been addressed explicitly, while outlining a few of the particularly difficult or important past, present, and future challenges facing the sociology of socialization, as defined in this book.

In order to focus on these questions in detail, I look, in turn, at the three most commonly studied variables in intersectional approaches, examined in reverse order compared to how much space they have each been given so far in the book. I begin with race (discussed in greater detail than the others, since it has received less direct analysis until now), before moving on to gender (and also briefly sexuality), and concluding with an issue that relates more (although not exclusively) to social class and that draws the book to a close where it began, looking at children and childhood.

1. What is racial socialization?

Class and gender socialization, discussed at length in earlier chapters, can be defined as the way in which material conditions of existence and experiences linked to a person's position in the social space of class and gender produce dispositions to act and to think in particular ways, which that person shares with some individuals and which are distinct from those of other groups. Similarly, occupying different positions within the social space of race also has effects on the "type of individual" we become.

What constitutes racial socialization? Through what agents does it operate and with what dispositional results? American sociology has long examined racial socialization, but primarily from one angle alone: education about race and racism (epitomized by "the talk" Black parents have with their children about racism, about the dangers they face as a result of it, and about how to handle interactions with authority figures, especially the police). While this approach has yielded many results, there still remains further potential to be drawn from the concept of socialization as defined in this book. Our first challenge here is therefore to construct racial socialization as a subject of study that includes these explicit, educational dimensions but that also extends beyond them, whilst equally taking into account the role played by the incorporation of dispositions, the unintentional, unconscious effects of this socialization, and the somatization of the social world. Such an approach can be broken down into two main components: studying socialization "to" race, on the one hand, and studying socialization "through" race, on the other.

1.1 Becoming aware of race (or not)

What makes up racial socialization? A first set of components concerns processes (some conscious and explicit, others unconscious and silent) of socialization to a racialized identity and to views of self and of the world engendered by a particular position within the social space of race.

1.1.1 Socialization to race and racism

Some of these processes have been studied, particularly since the 1980s in the United States, under the label "racial socialization" (sometimes referred to as "ethnic-racial socialization" [Hugues et al. 2006]). It is noteworthy that this is one of the rare areas in which the term "socialization" has continued to be used in English-language publications rather than following the general trend in which the notion has been discredited as obsolete (Guhin et al. 2021).

In these investigations and studies, racial socialization refers to educational processes (usually within the family) relating to racial identities and to racism. They address (1) the ways in which individuals construct their ethnic-racial identities in the sense of their feeling of belonging to an ethnic-racial group (including the way in which whites become aware [or not] of their whiteness and its associated advantages), and (2) how individuals become aware of the existence of race and racism, how members of ethnic-racial minorities learn to deal with racism and discrimination, and how individuals internalize racist prejudices.

In this kind of research, family socialization is most often considered as education – a set of "messages" that parents transmit to their children about race, such as the "lessons" they give them on the matter – and as "race-related communications" (Priest et. al. 2014; Hagerman 2014). The term "socialization" is used in ways that place emphasis on these educational and even strategic dimensions: "families also practice different socialization strategies in bringing up their children with respect to ethnicity" (Cheng and Kuo 2000: 467). As for the children, they are studied either from the perspective of developmental psychology and the stages at which racial identification appears or, conversely, in "socialization" approaches, in terms of childhood agency and creativity (Van Ausdale and Feagin 1996), notions to which we will return towards the end of the chapter. They "receive racial socialization messages from several sources" and this socialization is taken (in a very intellectualist fashion, focused on conceptions of race, racialized identities, etc.) to refer to the process through which "children come to understand their own and others' roles, identities, and positions vis-à-vis race" (Winkler 2011: 274), or to how, through "comprehensive racial learning," "children negotiate, interpret, and make meaning of the various and conflicting messages they receive about race, ultimately forming their own understandings of how race works in society and their lives" (Winkler 2012: 7).

A 2006 review, published in the journal *Developmental Psychology* (Hugues et al. 2006) and drawing on studies based on very diverse materials (statistical studies of opinions and practices, interviews, ethnographies, and so on), talks about the mechanisms through which parents transmit information, values, and perspectives on race and ethnicity, and the different forms that ethnic-racial socialization can take in the family. The article identifies four principal forms, all constructed from the point of view of the educating parents:

(1) Cultural socialization: transmitting culture (values, knowledge, practices) and encouraging its appreciation (telling children about their culture and its history, celebrating its holidays, cooking its traditional meals, encouraging children to speak its language, and so on).

(2) Preparation for bias: making efforts to prepare children for the discrimination they will face (making them aware of prejudice and enabling them to anticipate it).

(3) Promotion of mistrust: giving value to mistrust and promoting caution, or even distance, in interracial interactions.

(4) Egalitarianism: expressing an explicit preference for egalitarianism or being silent about race relations (emphasizing individual qualities rather than membership of racial groups, directing children's practices and values towards those of mainstream dominant social groups, i.e. "mainstreaming" or "mainstream socialization").

The forms of socialization identified in these kinds of surveys are very useful for identifying the processes at work, but the approach remains limited to analyzing statements about practices made from the point of view of parents. Moreover, with a process as complex as socialization, it is questionable whether such reviews can truly provide any fine-grained analysis of the different forms of socialization to race relations, and above all whether general conclusions (for example in terms of class and gender) can be drawn from so many studies with such varied methodologies and aims. We can perhaps gain more insight into how, and to what extent, parents teach their children to be aware of race relations, to tackle them or avoid them, to be proud of their ethnic-racial identity or not, and so on, by focusing in detail on certain specific examples, whether or not they draw explicitly on the notion of racial socialization itself. This approach could also then provide the basis for further quantitative studies that would be both more homogeneous and better adjusted to examining socialization.

Of course, these learning processes are not independent from other positions in the social space, for example within class relations. To illustrate this, let us return to our two empirical examples from Chapter 1 on Black masculinities and focus on the processes of racial socialization in play. Ann Arnett Ferguson's study of twenty fifth- and sixth-grade African American boys highlighted class variations in socialization to race. In all the families, Black masculinity is produced in a "context of social terror that arises out of a group condition," and "all the families prepare their sons to inhabit a world in which they are in danger – an 'endangered species' – and inculcate them with forms of defense and survival" (2000: 133). However, Ferguson's research also identifies a distinction among these working-class families between two kinds of socialization depending on the families' specific social positions. As we saw in Chapter 1, while all the parents of young Black males in her study worry about their sons' safety, they pass on different kinds of "survival strategies" to their children. In the lower-middle-class families where parents believe their children can achieve upward social mobility through education, strategies of "racelessness" and "avoidance" are encouraged and children are taught to control themselves and not fight back. Conversely, in the poorer families where the parents feel powerless when it comes to protecting their children from the realities of the world, the children learn to stand up for themselves and to engage in confrontation (107). We can see here how these two kinds of socialization "to race" are embedded in the different social positions and worldviews that account for them. We can also see – and we will return to this later – that it is not only ideologies and values but also dispositions that are incorporated during a process of socialization "through race," that is to say socialization produced by a position in the social space of race, but also by material conditions of existence and repeated practices and everyday experiences that are embedded in race relations and the dynamics of domination.

At the other extreme of the social space, Lawrence Otis Graham begins his study of the Black upper classes by recounting that, throughout his childhood, he thought there were only two types of Black people: those who passed the "brown paper bag and ruler test" (1999: 1) and those who didn't; in other words, those whose skin was darker than the bag and whose hair was less straight than the ruler. In his own case, his "complexion was a shade lighter than the brown paper bag" but his hair had a kink that made it "the antithesis of ruler-straight." He does not just mention the existence of this symbolic racial boundary, he also suggests a possible source for how he came to internalize it, pointing to the summers that he and his brothers spent in the late 1960s with his great-grandmother, a "well-educated, light-complexioned, straight-haired black southern woman" (1) from an upper-middle-class family. She forbade them from spending too much time in the sun, lest it darken their skin – "God knows you're dark enough already" (2) – and supervised them from the porch of her luxury summer home in Martha's Vineyard, only stepping inside to seek out her brush and comb when she "thought about her hair," still checking from afar that the children were not going to play in the sun. According to Graham, the strength and repetitive nature of these practices meant that, by age six, he already knew the importance of "achieving a better shade of black" (4) and that Blacks were divided into "us" and "them," "our kind of people" and the others (4–5).

This striking example offers material for a wealth of analyses on racial categories, identities, and identifications, in which, as Graham constantly reminds the reader, social class and race relations are intertwined ("it was a color thing and a class thing" [4]). From our perspective, however, moving away from the *existence* of these categories per se, we can look instead at the *processes* that enable their internalization: Graham's great-grandmother's explicit educational practices, but also all the silent socialization emanating from her own relationship to the world that was transmitted unconsciously when she read the magazine *Ebony* and commented upon its contents in front of her great-grandchildren, or when she straightened her own hair.

These two ethnographic studies give an idea of the processes and class variations involved in this socialization "to race" in which racial boundaries and social race relations are incorporated and/or explicitly addressed. But even practices and discourses that are not explicitly racialized can constitute ethnic-racial socialization, fostering, for example, pride in one's race or ethnicity, or skills to fight discrimination, as shown by a study focusing on the educational and leisure practices of middle-class British people of varied ethnic-racial origin. Arguing that practices of "concerted cultivation" as analyzed by Lareau (and discussed in Chapter 1) are affected by race, the authors show that, for middle-class Black Caribbean-heritage parents, enrolling their children in a host of extra-curricular activities is also a way of arming them against racism, by making them proud of their ethnic-racial belonging and by giving them skills and qualities that will be useful in the professional world – something of which the parents expect their children to have particular need in light of the disadvantages and discrimination they are likely to face (Vincent et al. 2013). Socialization "to race" therefore also operates through practices or in areas in which it is neither explicit nor always even conscious, and it therefore cannot simply be reduced to racial messages, communication, and education.

1.1.2 Socialization to dominant positions in the social space of race
While most American research examining "racial socialization" since the 1980s has tended to study how the parents of non-white children prepare them to live in a racially divided world, socialization to race is not something experienced only by children who are Black or from ethnic minorities in general (Hagerman 2016; 2018). As Connolly et al. (2009) have shown, since the 1920s numerous studies have focused on the socialization to racism – to racist prejudices or to exercising racism – that operates in white families (or more generally in families that hold dominant positions within the social space of race). An often-cited 1988 study looked at children's racial prejudice from the perspective of socio-cognitive developmental psychology and argued that it became strong and commonly accepted among white children between the ages of four and seven (Aboud 1988). Moreover, "white racial socialization" can also be identified,

in which white children either do or do not become aware of their position within the social space of race (and of their whiteness, specifically), of racism, and of "racial privilege" – even though studies show that most white parents neither talk about "race" nor recognize that they "belong" to a racial group. According to Margaret Ann Hagerman, there is, however, always a "racial context of childhood" (2014) that becomes operative through the "everyday choices that white parents make [that] shape how their children produce ideas about race, such as when to lock car doors, which friendships to encourage or discourage, whether and how to respond to questions posed by children, and so on" (Hagerman 2016: 62). She shows how, in affluent white families, there is explicit racial socialization – parents talk about (or do not talk about) racism with their children, especially after questions from the latter – but also implicit racial socialization: some parents enroll their children in an "integrated school" and thus create for them a "colour-conscious context," while others enroll them in exclusively white schools thus placing them in a "colour-blind context" (Hagerman 2014).

Hagerman (2016) has also examined the education that fathers who identify as "progressive" or "left-wing" seek to give to their children in order to raise them in an antiracist way, demonstrating how this produces both explicit and implicit white racial socialization. She shows that the fathers' educational intentions both challenge and reproduce hegemonic whiteness. As a result of their dominant position in the social space of both race and class, the fathers believe they can entirely control their children's environment and thus promote interracial interactions. However, they can also use that position to back out of situations they find "too racist" and insulate their children from them, thus reproducing (and perhaps transmitting, although Hagerman does not analyze this aspect) a dominant relationship to racial integration, or even racial stereotypes. Whereas studies in developmental psychology focus on children's representations, these sorts of investigations can reveal how processes of socialization to racial identity are caught up in everyday educational practices, school strategies, and sociability.

1.2 Incorporating "race"

I could leave the topic of racial socialization here, having explored different dimensions of the processes involved. But from the perspective adopted in this book, socialization is more than the either deliberate or unconscious internalization of conceptions of self and others, ways of viewing the world and more specifically social relations. When we talk about "class" socialization or "gender" socialization, we mean the way in which an individual's position in the social space of class or gender produces a particular type of person, particular dispositions, a particular habitus. This relates not only to how that person views their position, how they identify with a certain kind of femininity or masculinity, whether they feel ashamed or proud of their class background, or how they approach relationships with members of other social classes, but also to how this particular position constructs a particular individual with a body, tastes, and practices that are, in part, the result of that position. So what of "racial socialization" from this perspective?

Ethnic-racial socialization can be defined as the process through which different ethnic and racial groups transmit and internalize or incorporate specific ways of acting, thinking, and perceiving that are distinct from those of other groups. In addition to socialization "to race," there is therefore also socialization "through race," that is to say a form of socialization that is determined by one's position in the social space of race and that informs more than just how one views oneself and others, that in fact creates particular dispositions and particular individuals. These processes are conceptually distinct from those just analyzed in that they are largely unconscious, they are incorporated, and they generate different products (namely, dispositions, habitus, and individuals, rather than just conceptions, representations, and views of the world). Here, as elsewhere in the book, this is about the enduring ways in which social experiences are inscribed upon the body and how they go on to determine not only ways of seeing the world but also practices, or even, to cite Wacquant, how

> a system of ethnoracial classification – a taxonomy trading on the overt or covert correspondence between social and

natural orderings – is created and inculcated, sedimented in the socialized body in the form of the ethnic habitus, and mapped onto a system of ethnoracial *stratification* through the differential distribution of material and symbolic goods, privileges and penalties, profits and perils, across social and physical space. (2022: 87)

The idea is not to replace one approach (classic racial socialization) with another (socialization through incorporation), but rather to apply the general approach of the sociology of socialization to this particular area. In order to address race in terms of dispositional incorporation, it is therefore necessary to detach the sociology of race from an exclusive focus on the "sociology of identity," which, historically, served as a counterpoint when socialization through incorporation was theorized. This can no doubt allow us better to conceptualize in empirical and scientific terms how race, gender, and class are interrelated, and apply this to the phenomena discussed here – particularly since it means analyzing all three types of social relations through the same lens.

School socialization (in which the agent at work is school, and more specifically the teachers as representatives of the institution) offers an example that highlights how, over time, racial assignations and the repeated, unconscious practices to which they give rise produce different attitudes and even different bodies among students. Michela Musto's very detailed study (2019) pays attention to a range of variations relating to academic level, gender, race, and class, and shows how in "lower-level courses, where non-affluent Latinx students were overrepresented, educators penalized" boys' rule-breaking and particularly interruptions, whereas "in higher-level courses, where affluent, White, and Asian-American students were overrepresented, educators tolerated" this behavior and sometimes even encouraged it. The teachers' repeated reactions to misbehavior varied according to the students and ultimately resulted in the students developing different attitudes as they progressively incorporated these experiences: the more affluent boys took up more and more space in the higher-level classes, while the girls lost confidence after two years of being pushed aside by the boys interrupting them (something that did not happen in lower-level classes). Meanwhile, in the lower-level classes, the Latinx boys gradually disengaged: "rather than participating as they once had, lower-level boys – especially those who repeatedly interrupted as 6th- and 7th-graders – now spent class time sitting slouched in their seats or with their heads on their desks." We can see how, through frequent, repetitive practices and experiences, racial assignations and categorizations come to produce different attitudes and even different bodies and physical postures. In the longer run, they also produce unequal trajectories both at and after school: a person's position in the social space of race is inscribed in the body and not just the mind, as we saw with Bourdieu in Chapter 1.

A particularly effective, and also rare, example of research focusing on racial socialization understood as the sociogenesis of specific dispositions can be found in Bourgois and Schonberg's 2007 study, on which I shall focus in detail here. Taking inspiration from their work, it is possible to describe the products of these processes of socialization as ethnically structured dispositions, or "ethnically patterned habitus" to use their exact terms. Studying the differentiated behavior of white and African American homeless drug addicts in San Francisco, Bourgois and Schonberg argue that

> the "ethnicized" dimensions of habitus that we have been observing ethnographically manifest themselves as distinct body postures, scarring patterns, disease infection rates, clothing style preferences, bathing practices, smell management, poly-drug consumption choices, mechanisms of drug administration, relationships to sexuality, income-generating strategies, family structures, and tenors of interpersonal relations. (2007: 9–10)

They reveal two systems of recurring differences between the white and African American homeless addicts in their study, analyzing these systems as "two components of ethnic habitus" and reconstructing their genesis and the structures through which they were incorporated.

The first example concerns "techniques of the body" governing (1) differentiated modes of heroin injection

– intravenous for the African Americans, leaving them more exposed to contracting HIV, and, for the whites, into body fat or muscle tissue, sometimes through their clothes, making them particularly vulnerable to abscesses; and (2) differences in the sensations sought – an "exhilarating rush of pleasure" for the former, versus routine satisfaction for the latter. These seemingly trivial differences in fact play a structural role in producing different bodies and different diseases and are themselves ethnically structured. The African American addicts in the study continue to be concerned with their corporeal appearance, in terms of their dress but also their self-presentation more generally, and the authors link this to forms of masculinity forged during their past as gang members, as well as to the strong, active ties they maintain with their family and friends. The fact that they "persevere in seeking the pleasure of an exhilarating high" from drug use can also be related to this enduring concern for the self. Conversely, the white heroin addicts in the study had a more passive, dejected demeanor and displayed more apathetic dispositions and techniques of the body. They had given up on personal bodily care, which the authors linked to the fact that they had no available or internalized models of masculinity from prior gang membership, were entirely cut off from their families, and were treated like pariahs by the working-class communities from which they originated. Their having given up on self-care and on the body as a source of satisfaction thus helps to explain the routine, apathetic mode in which they injected heroin. Structured differences between prior socialization – in the family, the peer group (particularly gangs for the African American addicts), or juvenile correctional facilities – are thus able to explain incorporated dispositions underpinning differentiated social uses of the body.

The second example analyzed by the authors concerns variations in income-generating strategies. The African American homeless in the study had more frequently been to prison as teenagers than the white homeless from comparable social backgrounds, thus developing a greater propensity to "identify themselves in a celebratory manner as successful outlaws" and to obtain money through delinquent practices. Their position in the social space of race produced differentiated experiences in their teenage years and therefore differentiated socialization processes resulting in structural, determining dispositions that they shared with others from the same group and that differed from those of people in other groups. However, analysis of this example can extend beyond the scale of individual biography and show how "the memory of slavery is a sediment from history" that can explain these variations in income-seeking strategies (an argument reminiscent both of Bourdieu's comments about the body as a "memory pad" and of his use of Durkheim's idea of the "long period of the past" that we contain within us). Bourgois and Schonberg observe that the African American addicts prefer to steal than to beg or work as casual day laborers, and connect these dispositions to the memory of slavery (passed down and reinterpreted by their parents and grandparents who were immigrants from the Deep South, fleeing generalized racism and particularly high rates of lynchings) that leads them to see certain working conditions as "demeaning, exploitative, and feminizing":

> Concretely, the memory of slavery as a sediment from history manifests itself in the ways that unemployed African American drug users on the street experience humiliation around the kind of subordinated patron-client relationships that business owners impose on day laborers. The white homeless do not resonate with the same sense of outrage and insult at the hands of their often abusive part-time employers. (2007: 17)

Moreover, active, persisting racism on the part of the general public or the police also makes it harder for African Americans to rely on begging, thus "reactivating" ethnically structured dispositions from the past. The African Americans in the study consider it a choice not to beg (which they describe as "awkward" or "boring" [23]) and are unaware that this choice is socially structured, seeing it instead as an individual stance that preserves their dignity. As Bourgois and Schonberg put it, "these contrasts between African Americans and whites are not merely enduring cultural traits. The critical analytical purpose of the concept of habitus is dissipated if we lose sight of the generative forces in the crucible of symbolic power relations that produce cultural repertoires" (28). A person's position within race relations does not just produce differences that are habitually described as "cultural" – preferences, traditions, a "culture" as something that *one possesses* or *believes one is* and that serves as a reference – but also bodies, tastes, and inclinations, which can be unconscious and still play a highly determining role. These factors can affect extremely varied areas of practice and their sociogenesis can be pieced together or outlined: this is something one *is* because one has *been made that way*.

Defined in these terms, ethnic-racial socialization constitutes an almost entirely unexplored area of research, since the sociology of racial socialization takes a different approach (and does not consider things in terms of dispositions), and the sociology of socialization conceived as the incorporation of dispositions has so far only focused rarely on race.

Of course, the incorporation approach does not in any way invalidate or replace the studies on racial socialization discussed earlier. It simply takes a different perspective on the same phenomena, addressing them as ethnically structured and structuring, socially determined, and in part unconscious, and considering that their genesis can be traced back to more than just declarations of intent or explicit educational programs. In order to achieve a more fine-grained understanding of the links between socialization "to race" and socialization "through race," we can observe how racialized "schemes of perception" or "dispositions to believe" racial prejudice are incorporated. This is at least partly how racist bias is internalized, as demonstrated by a study on the way children acquire "ethnic attitudes and identities in contexts where ethnicity is not marked by physical differences" (Connolly et al. 2009: 217). The study shows that, from a very early age, young children in Northern Ireland prefer the cultural features associated with their ethnic group (Catholic or Protestant). As early as three to six years old, they prefer the colors of "their" flag rather than the other (the Irish flag or the British Union flag), like either Catholic or Protestant first names more, and a greater proportion of Catholic children than Protestant children state that they do not like the police (who tend to be viewed as Protestant allies). The study argues that the learning processes analyzed are largely unconscious. The children acquire these preferences before being aware of the conflict structuring the society they live in and before having a conscious sense of belonging to one of the two ethnic groups. The authors use the expression "ethnic habitus" to emphasize that these perceptions are "taken for granted" and are just as much, if not more, the result of unconscious incorporation as of explicit education. This therefore sheds light on "the complex ways" in which ethnicity is "acquired by young children and expressed through the way they come to 'talk, feel and act' [...] largely without any understanding or awareness of why they prefer certain cultural events and symbols over others" (220).

This line of research can also involve studying demeaning racial prejudices, including among members of minorities. For example, Frances Aboud's landmark study (1988) on children's racial bias argues that as soon as the first racial prejudices appear, white children are systematically negative towards members of other groups, whereas children from minorities display more heterogeneous attitudes and some are more negative towards members of their own group. Flicking through her magazine, commenting on each photograph, Lawrence Otis Graham's great-grandmother, mentioned earlier in this chapter, taught her great-grandchildren to look down upon Black people with the wrong complexion or with hair that was not straight enough. Similarly, many of the Black upper-class children Graham describes in his book attended elite private schools where the only other Black person to be found was the custodian. More fundamentally, Great-Grandmother Porter also taught them to read skin color or hair type as key social markers, assessed according to minute gradations, offering a clear, direct expression of social excellence. Socialization to race is therefore always socialization through race, that is to say a learning process that is situated in a hierarchically structured social space.

One final study shows how the two processes – socialization to race, incorporation of race – can pull individuals in different directions. Neda Maghbouleh's analysis focuses on two generations of Iranian Americans in California and seeks to link together the sociology of immigration and the sociology of race relations. The parents of her respondents were all "intensely socialized into a white Iranian national narrative" (2017: 57) and even into seeing themselves as "Aryan" and anti-Arab. The young Iranian Americans in the study all therefore grew up in homes where they were told time and time again, whether implicitly or explicitly, that they were white. It would therefore follow that this education about, or socialization to, race would lead them to think of themselves as white – which they in fact are as far as official federal categories are concerned. However, this is not what happened over the course of their lives. On the contrary, in Los Angeles (where certain houses in the wealthy neighborhood of Beverly Hills are described as "Persian" monstrosities because of their "impure" architectural style) and above all at school and at university, the respondents experienced racialization and stigmatization on a daily basis. They were subject to remarks or even insults about their skin color, eyebrows and hairiness, "bizarre" names, and bilingualism, as well as about their origins, which were viewed as "dubious" in post 9/11 America. This produced an enduring racial self-awareness as they incorporated a dominated position within the social space of race. This was not the position their parents had taught them or, more precisely, had sought to instill in them: they believed they were quite obviously not white ("I never considered myself white [...] I just *know* we're not white" [60]), felt insecure and illegitimate in terms of their physical appearance (after recounting how she was told she had a unibrow and was so hairy she was "like a gorilla," one respondent remarked "I would be like 'OK dude I know. Thanks for the reminder'" [50]), and had a sense of cultural illegitimacy. They did not, for example, feel able to represent the school's white students, as evidenced by the exception when one of the respondents managed to overcome this and run for president of her elementary school in fifth grade, thus "choosing to render herself visible and legible in front of her fifth-grade class" (88). The boys engaged in specific body work to prepare for going through security checks in American airports (shaving very closely, hesitating about which clothes or accessories would seem less "Middle Eastern," which books to put in their bags or not, etc.). As Maghbouleh puts it, this second generation "becom[es] brown by choice and by force" (172) as a result of "everyday experiences of racialization" (2) and "embodied micro-interactional experiences" (112), of state surveillance and media representations, and even of learning from agents other than their parents or federal categories "that it's not only okay but also vital to align with other liminal and highly racialized groups, including Arab Americans" (12).

The specificity of this position "at the limits of whiteness" could be seen as a form of secondary socialization to minority positions, following on from primary socialization to whiteness. However, it seems more accurate and more productive to see it as a manifestation of the existence of the incorporation of race and the strength with which it produces dispositions and thus individuals – even when this runs counter to parental education or federal categories, with socialization "through race" following on from education about race/socialization "to race." Thinking about education and incorporation together, understanding socialization in action and not just through its finished products, and conceiving of racial socialization as something that unfolds over the life course (as in other areas of practice) are fundamental challenges that the sociology of socialization must address.

1.3 Dealing with the difficulties of this approach

Empirical studies of the sociogenesis of ethno-racial dispositions and habitus remain relatively few and far between. Furthermore, this conception of racial socialization does not come without its difficulties, some of which are similar to the challenges facing analyses of other types of social relations and some of which are specific to the issue of race.

First of all, there is an obvious risk of what could be called "re-naturalization." One of the strengths of approaches focusing on habitus or dispositions is that they show that the habitus is a "second nature" and that conditions of existence and experiences construct both dispositions that are resistant to change and bodies that experience themselves as self-evident. There is always a risk, however, of "re-naturalizing" this second nature when its conditions of incorporation are overlooked (either in the way research is used or even in the research itself) or when it is argued that the ethnic-racial dispositions or socialization processes being described concern the group as a whole and are identical for all members of that group. Referring to "Latinx" dispositions, to the "white" habitus, or to "Asian" socialization implies making a generalization about dispositions and socialization across the whole group, which risks not only producing oversimplified or even erroneous readings but also perpetuating and reifying stereotypes. These are not new problems for the sociology of socialization (does the "feminine habitus" referred to in Bourdieu's *Masculine Domination* truly exist?) and they require the sociologist always to analyze the socialization of a given ethnic-racial group as creating differences between one group and another, rather than characterizing all members of that group, just as with Bourdieu's class habitus (see Chapter 1). Moreover, it is important to offer an account of the sociogenesis of the "second nature" in question, so as not to forget that it is both socially constructed and embedded in a historical context. As Bourgois and Schonberg remind us:

> A straightforward phenomenological description of the effects of habitus risks reifying stereotypes around culture [of the type] "niggers are thieves" [or] "whites are lame no hustles who lack self-respect and initiative." In order to open the black box of habitus and de-essentialize the existence of these patterns in everyday interactions at the level of individuals, we need to look at the generative forces of habitus formation. To denaturalize the practices and the forms of embodiment that are associated visibly with ethnicity, we need to relate habitus to the structures of symbolic power that give it meaning. (2007: 15–16)

A second difficulty lies in the problems inherent to approaches that consider how the dominated may participate in their own domination. These problems have been clearly identified in the case of both gender and class socialization (see, for example, the criticisms leveled against the idea of consent to domination in Bourdieu's texts on masculine domination and in the debates around the notion of the "culture of poverty" [Small et al. 2010; Bettie 2003: 118–20]). This is also obviously a sensitive issue when it comes to racial socialization. The question of domination intersects with discrimination and sociological approaches to the latter do not engage with the question of whether those being discriminated against participate in that discrimination, while, in the political and judicial spheres, there is the added importance of avoiding "victim-blaming." Rather than eschewing an approach whose specificity is precisely that it tracks domination across the social world as a whole – including in the minds and bodies of the dominated – it is perhaps instead worth taking particular care in *how* we do this work. This could mean, for example, taking a systematically symmetrical approach that never focuses solely on how the dominated act against their own interests (i.e. suggesting that, through their conduct, they are somehow complicit in their own domination), but that always examines the actions of the dominant as well, and always considers how domination is reproduced by everyone involved. Another useful principle could be always to seek to *show* the socializing principles underpinning behavior, rather than simply referring to them. Far from being responsible for victim-blaming, socialization could then serve as a useful tool for analyzing actors' situations and points of view, without elitism or judgment, and for offering a scientifically, but also ethically and politically, sound way of analyzing individuals in dominated positions within different social relations.

Finally, a more methodological or theoretical difficulty must also be considered, namely the way in which different variables can be conflated or, on the contrary, artificially separated. Taking a class/gender/racial socialization approach consists in isolating, or demarcating, certain types of disposition by ascribing their genesis to a particular position in class/gender/race relations. While this is theoretically possible, it can be empirically difficult: can we always "isolate" one particular sociogenesis from another? Can we really determine which dispositions "come from" positions relating to gender, class, or race, when we know that all these processes operate together from a specific position defined by all these different dimensions? On the other hand, invoking the fundamental intersectionality of each position runs the reverse risk of remaining theoretical or abstract and can also hinder analysis in the chemical sense of the term, as Bourdieu would put it – that is, the process through which each element is separated out and examined in its own right – which remains a fundamental tool for objectivation. Where class and gender are concerned, sociologists of socialization tend to manage, albeit not without difficulty, to separate them out and to identify the production of class-situated masculinities and femininities, on the one hand, and of feminine and masculine versions of class socialization on the other. This suggests that it must also be possible, and would certainly be desirable, to do the same thing for race; in other words, to keep in mind the need to understand how different relations of domination "work together" whilst at the same time analyzing the specific effects of a given position within the social space of race.

2. Doing gender or being done by gender?

The answer to the question of whether we do gender or are done by gender could be "both, of course," and this would certainly offer an easy way to dispense with it. The challenge, however, lies in understanding how the two intersect and in determining what kind of sociology of gender socialization would be required to address both and thus respond to the criticisms that have been levied against socialization in this area, where it has clearly fallen out of favor. Gendered behaviors are now largely studied either in terms of performance and the idea of "doing gender" (West and Zimmerman 1987; West and Fenstermaker 1995) or in terms of the embodiment of (e.g. hegemonic) masculinity or femininity (Connell 2005). Can the sociology of gender socialization bring anything more to the table than simply a return to the social and sociological world of the 1950s?

2.1 Moving away from gender socialization?

Without entering into the details of the two main approaches to gendered behaviors, let us briefly review the criticisms of socialization that each has formulated and how their theoretical proposition differs from it. The ethnomethodological approach of "doing gender" was explicitly constructed as an alternative to the "received doctrine of gender socialization theories" that, according to West and Zimmerman, "conveyed the strong message that while gender may be achieved, by about age five it was certainly fixed, unvarying, and static – much like sex" (1987: 126). To remedy this form of (re)naturalization, the "doing gender" approach proposed an understanding of gender "as an accomplishment, an achieved property of situated conduct" that locates gender not in individuals but in the social situations in which they live their lives. From this perspective, the scientific focus, that is to say the construction of "gender" as an object of study, shifts from "matters internal to the individual" to "interactional, and ultimately institutional, arenas" (126). Gender is thus an "emergent feature of social situations," an ongoing activity embedded in, and created and recreated by, everyday interactions. It is therefore located "outside" individuals even though they are the ones who "do" gender. Within this approach, the "socialization" view of gender is criticized for individualizing and re-naturalizing gender by making it into an internal, unchanging attribute that is fixed in childhood, and for failing to take into account the effect of interactions or institutions on how gender is constructed and on how it can evolve. How can the sociology of socialization respond to the challenges represented by these criticisms?

The first point to make is that one of the aims of the dispositionalist approach to socialization is precisely to consider together, rather than in opposition, the individual on the one hand, and interactions, institutions, and social situations on the other. In the theory of habitus and its sociogenesis, social structures always exist simultaneously in the social world and in the individual in their internalized form. The socialization approach does examine the "individual traits" produced by gender socialization, which might seem to correspond to the criticisms it faces from the "doing gender" camp. However, it analyzes these traits as the product of interactions, institutions, social situations, and experiences – a set of components that are all taken into account in the "doing gender" approach too. Rather than "individualizing" gender, the socialization approach seeks to understand it both inside and outside the individual, looking at how it is internalized (through varied socialization processes, as we have seen throughout this book) and how it is externalized (in gendered practices that result from the gendered dispositions that have been internalized). This is what Bourdieu describes as the "dialectic of the internalization of externality and the externalization of internality" (1977: 72). Finally, for Bourdieu, social space is a *relational* space and it is the *relative* positions of individuals and groups within that space that produce a given type of socialization. Socialization therefore contains this relational aspect "within it," as it were, even when expressed in individual dispositions.

Furthermore, as we have also seen throughout this book, the dispositionalist approach to socialization is not limited to the idea that everything plays out in early childhood – a point of view decried by the "doing gender" approach. On the contrary, it seeks to analyze socialization as a process that unfolds over the life course and that is in no way fixed, unvarying, or static. It does, however, make it possible to take into account the non-variable, fixed elements that do exist, especially in gender socialization, which, as we saw in the previous chapter, is very often reinforced throughout the life course. This aspect is much harder to integrate in the "doing gender" approach, with its (perhaps somewhat artificial?) idea that gender is reinitialized in each interaction. Similarly, the "doing gender" approach has long struggled to take into account other forms of power relations and the effects of other aspects of social structure, such as class (West and Fenstermaker 1995), which socialization approaches, in contrast, are well-equipped to grasp.

A second point to be made is that the "doing gender" approach does not in fact resolve the problem of socialization, which remains a blind spot, and one on which the dispositional approach can shed productive light. West and Zimmerman's founding article concludes with the following research agenda (which, incidentally, was neither fulfilled nor renewed in West and Fenstermaker's later 1995 article): "To bring the social production of gender under empirical scrutiny, we might begin at the beginning, with a reconsideration of the process through which societal members acquire the requisite categorical apparatus and other skills to become gendered human beings" (1987: 140). Is this not precisely the task that the dispositionalist sociology of socialization, as defined in this book, proposes to tackle? Far from being an easy scapegoat, to be dismissed as outdated, the notion of socialization can in fact offer an account of how we learn to do the gender that we do, or how we have learned to want to do the gender that we do, sometimes consciously and sometimes unconsciously. The blind spot of "doing gender" approaches is in fact the focal point of the socialization approaches described in this book and opposing these two sociologies without taking into account the entirely different ways in which they construct their object of study makes little theoretical or scientific sense. However, both approaches have much to gain from considering each other's blind spots, and the challenge for the dispositionalist sociology of socialization is therefore taking into account the social variations in how gender is produced throughout the life course, as well as the ways in which interactions and situations activate, reactivate, or inhibit incorporated dispositions.

Gender socialization as an ongoing process (rather than as a set of results crystallized in bodies, identities, or sex roles) is also to some extent a blind spot in another key approach taken to gender today, namely Raewyn Connell's notion of hegemonic masculinities and of the embodiment of masculinities and femininities more broadly. Connell's theoretical standpoint was also, to some extent, developed "against" the "sex roles" and "socialization" approaches. According to her, by analyzing things like the "male sex role," these approaches engage in "categorical thinking persistently underplaying diversity within the gender categories" and are therefore reifying, naturalizing, and unable to take into account material conditions of existence and power relations (Connell 1985). Connell offers a way of breaking "with the unified vision of masculinity produced by the functionalist and analytically unsatisfactory" notion of "sex roles" and of reconciling the idea of a dominant ("hegemonic") form of masculinity ("the" masculine, in the singular) with the recognition that masculinity, more generally, comes in multiple forms and embodiments ("masculinities" in the plural) (Bertrand et al. 2015). Hegemonic masculinity is the one that, at a given moment in time or in a given social space, "embodies the currently accepted answer to the problem of the legitimacy of patriarchy, which guarantees (or is taken to

Race, Gender, Children's Agency   159

guarantee) the dominant position of men and the subordination of women" (Connell 2005: 77).

In some of its expressions, Connell's sociology could seem quite close to the dispositionalist sociology of gender socialization, for example when she defines "masculinity" as "simultaneously a place in gender relations, the practices through which men and women engage that place in gender, and the effects of these practices in bodily experience, personality and culture" (2005: 71). As a set of practices, masculinity does indeed have effects on "bodily experience, personality, and culture," but the question of the individual sociogenesis of this "structure of social practice" is once again not addressed in this approach to gender and only touched upon briefly (by Connell, in responses to critiques of the notion of "hegemonic masculinity") in abstract and programmatic terms:

> Life-history research has pointed to another dynamic of masculinities, the structure of a project. Masculinities are configurations of practice that are constructed, unfold, and change through time. A small literature on masculinity and aging, and a larger one on childhood and youth, emphasize this issue. The careful analysis of life histories may detect contradictory commitments and institutional transitions that reflect different hegemonic masculinities and also hold seeds of change. (Connell and Messerschmidt 2005: 852)

As with the "doing gender" approaches, then, Connell's theory of gender struggles to account for how individuals learn masculinities and femininities, and thus how individuals are acted upon, determined, and constrained by them. Although, as we have seen, Connell does take a structural approach to masculine domination, which she views as a constraining social structure, she does not examine the processes through which this social structure is incorporated, leading in turn to the incorporation of types of masculinity and femininity not as choices, identities, or reflexivities but as bodies and corporeal habits, as tastes and distastes, as practices and viewpoints. At an individual level, masculinities (for example) are embodied, in the sense of being corporeal and displayed, but they are not incorporated, in Bourdieu's sense of the term, that is to say profoundly somatized during a process of socialization and structural in determining future behavior.[8] Gender is created by practices, but the individual matrix for these practices – that constitutes us as gendered subjects – is left aside or only mentioned in passing, as for example when Connell states that it is necessary to consider the social determinants of bodies and health, but without proposing any precise empirical approach for doing so (Connell 2012).

As we can see with these two examples, the sociology of socialization outlined in this book could be exactly what these different approaches to gender need in order to shed light on a common blind spot, namely the sociogenesis of the individuals who do gender or who embody masculinity and femininity – provided, of course, it manages to respond satisfactorily to criticism about reifying homogeneous, artificial gender "roles" and failing to take interaction and social change into account. This is why I argue in favor of explicitly linking together gender socialization and the idea of "doing gender" or gender as performance (one has to learn gender in order then to perform it) through the notion of incorporation (gender is performed because it is incorporated and not only embodied or displayed); in other words, we "do" gender because we are done by it, that is by male domination as a social structure.

2.2 A social space of socialization to styles of masculinity and femininity

Linking together the approaches of dispositionalist socialization and of hegemonic masculinity would also offer a better way of linking together class and gender socialization. The question of intersectionality is obviously just as essential for the sociology of socialization as for other sociological paradigms and, throughout this book, we have seen crossovers between different variables (although mainly two by two). It is important here to recall, as with race earlier, that for dispositionalist sociology the subject of study is not simply intersectional variations (for example, differences in practices and experiences, or categories and judgments, according to positions within the social space of class, gender, and race)[9] but also, and above all, the sociogenesis of dispositions that emerge from inhabiting a specific position at the intersection of various power relations. Moreover, while the sociology of socialization shares with other sociological approaches the requirement to grasp these different positions "at the same time" and to look at their "simultaneous effects" (West and Fenstermaker 1995: 33), it aims to do so empirically throughout.

A model that could link together Bourdieu's conception of "social space" with Connell's conception of "hegemonic masculinity" in the study of class and gender socialization would be the following: building out from Bourdieu's notion of the social space of class, each position in the space of social class could be said to determine the "style of masculinity" or the "style of femininity" to which one is socialized – along the same model as the "life-styles" that are determined by each class position according to Bourdieu's *Distinction*. Following this model, each position in the social space – defined by an overall quantity of capital, but also by the structure and make-up of the types of capital in question (cultural and economic, in particular) – then results in children internalizing particular styles of masculinity and femininity according to the sex ascribed to them when they were born. To take the example of masculinities, these "styles" would be class-differentiated ways of reproducing masculine domination: for example, a style of masculinity based on maintaining and valuing physical force in working-class backgrounds, one based on dominating the labor market in upper-class backgrounds with high levels of economic capital, and one based on soft skills and an egalitarian gender ideology in the middle and upper classes with high levels of cultural capital. Viewed in these terms, it could be argued that class socialization leads to the incorporation of styles of masculinity and femininity that are not just class variations but that are also socially varied ways of exercising, or being subjected to, masculine domination. The content of these styles of femininity and masculinity, as well as the processes through which they are incorporated, remain largely to be investigated, but this could certainly provide a fruitful avenue to be explored by a dispositionalist sociology of socialization looking to engage with the sociologies of both "doing gender" and of hegemonic masculinity. Taken

2.3 Are desires tastes that we acquire?

To conclude this focus on some of the challenges facing analyses of gender socialization, I would like briefly to consider the question of sexual socialization, which, as with the sociology of race, is made up of a dimension that has already been studied extensively from the perspective of education, and another dimension relating more to dispositions, which continues to pose a challenge and is a research agenda that remains to be defined.

The sentimental and sexual socialization produced by diverse agents operating in childhood and adolescence – the family, the media, peers, school – is now relatively well documented in its most explicit, educational dimension. For example, Karin Martin and Katherine Luke have shown the gendered nature of this sentimental and sexual socialization by observing "what mothers teach young children about sexuality and reproduction" and seeing that "mothers talk more to daughters than sons about romantic relationships, the workings of reproductive bodies, and moral issues around sexuality," but also that "the silence about the pleasurable aspects of sexuality is large for all children as discussions tend to be framed as about reproduction or danger" (Martin and Luke 2010).

We also know that socialization to heteronormativity takes place from a very early age (through the repeated and largely unconscious promotion not just of romance among children but specifically of heterosexual romance) and that the same is true for the incorporation of male power over female bodies. Observing this gendered sexual socialization in preschool classrooms, Heidi Gansen has shown how the school institution and its representatives serve as agents of sexual socialization, operating through the repetition of seemingly banal practices (such as not telling off – and perhaps even encouraging – a little boy who has kissed a little girl without asking her opinion, or excusing his behavior because he has a "crush" on her) that mean that children as young as three internalize the idea "that boys have gendered power over girls' bodies" (Gansen 2017).

However, unlike sentimental and sexual socialization, the sociogenesis of sexual tastes – whether for certain sexual practices or for partners of one sex or the other, for example – has received very little critical attention. Zerubavel mentions it in passing in his study of cognitive and sensory socialization, referring to the way in which, because of the categories to which they belong, we learn to see certain objects as "sexual" and able to generate desire, while others (such as "orchids"!) are not, "exemplifying the tremendous power of society to affect our taste, feelings, and moral senses by essentially controlling the gates to our minds" (1997: 52). However, the question of the sociogenesis of sexual desire has yet to be explored in any detail and even the theory of sexual scripts (according to which sexual scripts are something that we learn) remains closed to the question of how we learn desires and the processes that mean we come to desire a given type of person, a given sex or gender, and given sexual practices rather than others (Green 2008). There is therefore the potential for a new set of research avenues to be explored at the intersection of the dispositionalist sociology of socialization and the sociology of sexual desires, which could, for example, build out from the notion of "tastes," thus linking together Bourdieu's sociology of social space with the sociology of sexualities and sexual tastes.

3. What about children's agency?

In the previous section, we saw that many of the criticisms levied against socialization were in fact addressing ways of conceptualizing and using the notion that do not correspond to those put forward in this book. Other criticisms, however, do clearly target the approach discussed here: they argue that socialization approaches are too deterministic, that they do not make enough room for social change, and that they focus solely on socializing agents at the expense of the people actually being socialized, thereby failing to take individual agency into account. Since a considerable proportion of these kinds of criticisms have focused on children, I shall focus on this stage in socialization in order to outline the arguments and respond to them, thus ending the book where it began: with childhood.

Many studies in the sociology of childhood have criticized socialization approaches from the point of view of agency and autonomy, claiming that they ignore the children's point of view, frame them as putty in the hands of socialization processes that act upon them and through them, depriving them of any possibility of independent action, and overlook the ways in which children also "make themselves" through the peer socialization that constitutes an autonomous childhood culture (Corsaro 1992; Holloway and Valentine 2000; Chin and Phillips 2004). Regarding the latter point, we have already seen in Chapter 2 that the sociology of peer socialization does take these processes into account, whilst at the same time showing that they do not operate independently of other socializing agents such as school and parents, and that it is not productive to try to oppose these (parents versus peers, for example) as though they were entirely independent.

As for children's agency, my intention here is not to deny that it is valuable and even necessary to include this factor in the socializing equation, nor do I wish to deny the existence of children's own activities and own social being. However, it is worth underlining that claims about children's agency are sometimes more about theory and principle than about results. It is much easier to demonstrate that a given practice is the result of behavior learned via an agent of socialization than it is to demonstrate that it emerged freely and was *not* the result of socialization. To take a concrete example, when looking at children's summer holiday activities, it can seem as though children sometimes resist or evade their parents' educational endeavors (Chin and Phillips 2004), but even then, the things they choose to do instead (listening to the radio while pretending to work, playing computer games, etc.) are in themselves socially situated practices that may well be the result of class-determined tastes that they have internalized during family socialization. In general, it is much harder to prove that practices are non-determined than the reverse, and when the sociology of socialization tracks all the forms and effects of the learning processes that underpin practices, it more clearly meets the scientific requirements for proof and falsifiability than statements collated about the "free" nature of children's practices in which it is still entirely possible that these were learned from one source or another. As a consequence, the deterministic sociology of socialization could in fact be referred to as the true sociology of choices. Sociologists of socialization never stop at a given practice or taste and content themselves with deeming it "personal," "autonomous," or "free"; instead, they systematically try to open up the black box of choices, practices, and tastes in order to identify the many, minute factors that can explain them.

It is also worth bearing in mind the troubling similarities between this emphasis on children's agency and both contemporary educational norms promoting suspicion of any process that resembles indoctrination and the conceptions of childhood viewed as legitimate among the middle and upper classes (Lareau 2011; Kusserow 2004). Points of convergence include: the principle of strong continuity between childhood and adulthood (which could explain why sociologists are so keen to see children as social actors in their own right), a model of authority based on negotiation rather than obedience (which could explain why sociologists emphasize children's resistance and autonomy so much), and a form of soft individualism that insists upon the blossoming of children's faculties (which once again could explain sociologists' propensity to emphasize the autonomy of children's faculties). It is perhaps no coincidence that the scientific principles underpinning the decision to take into account children's agency are so similar to the prevailing conceptions of childhood in the researchers' own social space.

Finally, and above all, taking children's activities into account does not mean defining children as "actors" in their own socialization, as though they had mastered the socialization process so well that they were able to treat it as a "menu" from which they could pick and choose according to their desires – this is something that even adults cannot do, as far as the approach outlined in this book is concerned! A sociology of children that is attentive to social differentiation shows that children are not a homogeneous group, nor, above all, are they an autonomous group that produces "its own laws." And it is perfectly possible to take into account children's actions within the framework of a determinist and dispositional approach to socialization, as evidenced by Wilfred Lignier's work, whether on children at elementary school (with Julie Pagis) or on toddlers in a daycare center. Lignier shows that children are active and have competency, but equally that their actions and skills to some extent consist in *recycling* patterns or skills and resources they have incorporated as passive recipients of prior socialization processes. For example, children may draw on schemes of perception that come from school in their social relations with their peers (expressing the judgment "he gets bad grades" for example) and they may also classify occupations by drawing on values instilled in them by their parents (for example, "recycling" the instruction "don't touch that, it's dirty" into a principle according to which certain jobs are "dirty" and thus disparaged) (Lignier and Pagis 2017a; see also 2012; 2017b). In his study of toddlers, Lignier shows that those "who enjoy sufficient symbolic resources – a matter of age, class, and gender – are able to appeal to the authority of adults" (for example, asking for adult intervention when another child has taken something from them). They are also able to exert "immediate symbolic violence" in ways that are socially selective and that notably involve "the capacity to recycle the speech in which adults exercise authority in line with one's own practical goals, namely to actively reproduce a symbolic force that the toddlers had already experienced as passive objects of adult control" (Lignier 2021a: 246).

It would therefore be more accurate to talk about children being "active" during socialization insofar as the latter is the result of the encounter between the actions of the individuals in a position to socialize others and the actions of the individuals being socialized. Creating an opposition between deterministic conceptions of socialization and the agency of children as actors in their own right is particularly meaningless when we consider that the sociology of socialization can study how agency itself is learned and incorporated (since "human agency is clearly not given at birth" [Lignier 2021b: 201]). It can examine that process not only in general but also in its social variations and it can take into account how agency is manifested, whether in legitimate or illegitimate, profitable or non-profitable, forms. In his work on daycare centers, Lignier observed the day-to-day interactions between children and between children and their caregivers around ways of taking or giving objects, that is to say also ways of exercising or experiencing symbolic and practical forms of power. These practices are both socially differentiated and socially differentiating: children covet different things early on, in line with their social class and gender socialization; they have already learned – and they continue to learn – different ways to ask for them or to seize them by force; and, finally, their actions have different (and unequal) consequences in the daycare world where the legitimate way of taking possession of things is to ask for them, or where some children (socialized in middle- or upper-class families to the "right" ways to ask for or take possession of something) already have more power than others in defining what is desirable and in obtaining it: "agency not only results in power relations but also stems from them" (Lignier 2021b: 204). The sociology of socialization therefore clearly offers a way of taking children's agency into account and of analyzing it, by re-embedding it in social structures and power relations that extend beyond children's society. Contrary to its scientific reputation, the dispositionalist sociology of socialization therefore clearly seems able to take account of both agency *and* its social variations and the surrounding social structures, that is to say both individual activity *and* social inequalities.

This chapter has, I hope, completed my demonstration of what the sociology of socialization can bring to the table when it comes to analyzing contemporary society. The very particular sociological lens provided by the key concept of socialization is both resolutely empirical and effectively theoretical. It never engages in theory for theory's sake, treating it instead as a scientific tool that serves to explain empirical evidence. Socialization offers a way of accounting for the existence and intersectionality of different forms of domination and power relations – as we have seen here with the examples of race, gender, class, and age – by considering them at the level of the individual. It enables us to be attentive to the ways in which society produces different bodies and deep-seated desires, tastes, and distastes that we experience as individual choices because we have incorporated them as such. And it teaches us that our identities – with which we identify, upon which we reflect, which we manage and project into the world – are simply one aspect of the social construction of our being.

The socialization approach is not intended to replace existing sociological frameworks when it comes to analyzing the topics addressed in this chapter or any others. Instead, I would argue in favor of using socialization to broach questions that are not necessarily investigated by those frameworks because it can shed productive light on some of their blind spots. In the various cases discussed in this chapter, we have seen that the sociology of socialization encourages us always to take our analysis one step further. This means, for instance, not only examining explicit education about race when it comes to understanding racial socialization and not only identifying the effects that racism has on identity and self-perception, but also understanding how positions within the social space of race will produce different bodies and individuals. Similarly, it means not limiting ourselves to examining how gender is done in interactions and how this reproduces masculine domination, but also seeking to understand how the way in which we learn to do gender (and learn to *want* to do the gender that we do) determines how we behave in different situations and interactions. To take one final example, it means not explaining children's behavior solely in terms of children's agency and peer culture without at the same time seeking to identify their sources and influences, and going beyond the impression that they have appeared spontaneously or that they successfully resist adult impositions. In short, approaches focusing on socialization require us to look for empirical evidence of the origins of our dispositions to believe given things or to act in a given way. In doing so, they invite us more generally not to restrict our sociological lens from the outset and to give "sociogenetic" explanations a chance.

Finally, in addressing three types of challenges facing the sociology of socialization, this chapter has shown that the criticisms generally leveled against socialization are sometimes unjust or misplaced, often referring back to uses of the concept that differ from those outlined in this book. As our analytical pathway through the field of socialization draws to a close, the book's conclusion will now briefly outline some of ways in which it is possible to respond to these criticisms.

Conclusion

In his introduction to Durkheim's *Education and Sociology*, published in French in 1922, Paul Fauconnet, one of the author's disciples, defended the book's theory of socialization against the "resistance" with which it had met (Durkheim 1956: 31–3). A full century later, the notion of socialization is still meeting with resistance; perhaps more surprising still, the criticisms leveled against it today are remarkably similar to those of yesteryear. Fauconnet describes three types of resistance: a humanist objection accusing Durkheim of embedding socialization within local contexts (e.g. the nation) rather than approaching it at the level of humanity in general; a criticism of his realism, allegedly more intent on making fatalistic statements about how things are than on suggesting how things should be; and finally an individualist complaint that he dilutes the individual into society as a whole, whereas history suggests, on the contrary, that the freeing of the individual is "the dominant trait of the progress of civilization" (33). These criticisms are, respectively, political, epistemological, and historical, and the same is true of the following, more recent, objections that have been raised against socialization as a sociological approach.

First, political criticisms of the sociology of socialization argue that it posits the individual as "hypersocialized" in ways that run counter to the values of freedom and personal responsibility. Viewed from this perspective, the "conditioning" individuals undergo via socialization makes them into mere puppets under the control of a totalitarian society. This criticism therefore judges the descriptive endeavor of the socialization approach in light of ideological stakes, which is in itself questionable: after all, if we truly were entirely programmed automatons, would it not be better to know this rather than to act like Spinoza's drunkard, convinced that he is not in the slightest bit intoxicated and that he is in complete control of what he says and does? Moreover, it is difficult to ask science to demonstrate the existence of freedom, which is more experiential than it is tangible, whereas social conditioning and its products can meet the standards of proof on both the quantitative and the qualitative level. Furthermore, this criticism paints a particularly dark picture of socialization, whereas it is important to remember that socialization also underpins the physical and mental capabilities that we value in our democratic societies, not to mention the very importance we ascribe to notions such as freedom and the individual! Finally, this accusation sets aside the fact that sociological "determinism" is much less totalitarian than determinism in other disciplines: for example, unlike biological determinism (whether neuronal or genetic) sociologies of socialization may underline the strength of incorporation processes but they also emphasize the fact these are constructed, contextual, and embedded in history, as well as formed and transformed, and thus potentially transformable again.

Second, another set of criticisms make similar arguments but with an epistemological orientation. They contend that sociological approaches only taking socialization into account focus on only one parameter to the exclusion of all others, as though other potential principles underpinning individuals' actions do not exist. The allegedly ignored principles are often about rational, reflexive adaptation to the present situation, as opposed to the weight of the past pinning down the socialized individual. This objection presents the disadvantage of drawing a stark opposition between sociological theories that are not necessarily so diametrically opposed: the weight of the past versus the open-ended nature of the present, individual determinism versus interaction, socialization versus situation, and so on, whereas we have seen, for example, that the interactionist approach is perfectly capable of linking together the decisive role of situations and the deterministic dimension of socialization. Moreover, there is nothing about socialization that precludes taking into account the socialized individual's actions and room for maneuver, provided these are attested empirically and not just posited or invoked without substantiation. It is possible, for example, to ask to what extent individuals are aware of the socialization processes in which they are implicated, what techniques they can use to direct or change them (by removing themselves from certain influences or actively seeking out others), and whether there are forms of socialization in which the individual's room for maneuver is more pronounced than in others. Viewed in this way, agency is neither an act of faith nor a democratic belief, but rather a socially produced practice "like any other," structured according to social variations, requiring particular social conditions of possibility, and of which we can and should provide an account.

Finally, the last set of criticisms are more historical and individualist and perhaps the most reminiscent of the charges originally brought against Durkheim. Fauconnet's responses at the time therefore continue to offer an appropriate way to begin to respond to them now. The criticisms claim that the notion of socialization is not suited to sociological analysis of the contemporary world because it ignores the figure of the individual that that world has produced. As Fauconnet put it: "People are so accustomed to opposing society to the individual that every theory that makes frequent use of the word society seems to sacrifice the individual" (Durkheim 1956: 32). However, emphasizing the weight of society does not mean "sacrificing" the individual. We do not have to subscribe to the idea of a strict dichotomy between the "individual" and "society," which, as we have seen throughout this book, is not necessarily a productive opposition. Approaches in terms of socialization do not oppose society to the individual any more than they would oppose a folded up piece of paper to that same sheet of paper when it is smoothed out. They view society and the individual as two sides of the same coin, focusing on society as it has come to be crystallized in individuals and seeking to piece together the genesis of that process. They consider how the individual internalizes society

Conclusion 173

but also produces it through the externalization of internalized dispositions. Socialization is that which *builds* the individual and thus, I might add, it is the strength, continuity, and multiplicity of the processes through which it does so that ultimately produce individual singularity. Socialization is not limited to what is common to all members of a given society; it also extends to what is most individual in each member. It is therefore an analytical tool that is in fact particularly well-suited to the era of the individual.

The criticisms outlined here are even less warranted when we consider that the notion of socialization actually offers a way of examining the genesis of individuals that is politically open, epistemologically ambitious, and historically aware of the individual dimension of social processes. Finally, in the particular way it is understood in this book, socialization proves a particularly salient tool for taking into account power relations and inequalities, at the level of both social structures and individuals, as well as for taking into account the power of society to construct our bodies and our lives.

Notes

1 Throughout this book, Bourdieu's term *incorporation* in French has been rendered by "incorporation" rather than by "embodiment," which is often used in English-language translations or discussions of his work. Although the notion of the body (*"corps"* in French) is perhaps less immediately evident in incorporation in English (albeit present in the root), it seems to us – author and translator – that the word places greater emphasis on the process of "taking in" or "integrating" something, on the way in which the social environment "gets under the skin" and actually becomes part of the individual and their body. Moreover, it avoids giving the impression that *"incorporation"* is simply an "external" display, as can be the case with embodiment. This slightly estranging use of incorporation in English also presents the advantage of reflecting the specificity of Bourdieu's analytical framework vis-à-vis the way the notion of embodiment is used in various English-language theoretical propositions (e.g. in Raewyn Connell's or Nancy Krieger's work).
2 On the following passages, see also Darmon 2017, pp. 189–227.
3 Unless otherwise indicated, all translations of citations from texts published in French are my own (trans. note).
4 The analyses taken up here are those in chapter 3 of Berger and Luckmann's book.
5 Regarding the meaning of "alternation" that Berger used instead of conversion, with a view to employing a more "neutral" term without religious connotations, Richard Travisano (1970) suggests making a distinction between conversion and

alternation, the latter being a less radical change somewhat closer to what I refer to as "transformation" in this chapter.
6 See, for example, Strauss 1977, pp. 118–23.
7 In my own research, I have tried to apply this approach to anorexia (Darmon 2017), elite educational institutions (Darmon 2013), and post-stroke hospital rehabilitation (Darmon 2021).
8 As mentioned earlier, in order to account for the specificity of Bourdieu's notion of *incorporation* (in French), it has been translated by "incorporation" throughout this book rather than by "embodiment," as is sometimes the case.
9 American sociology has examined in some detail the intersectionality of class, gender, and race in studies on young people, but from the point of view of performance and identities rather than socialization. See, for example, Bettie 2003, Morris 2008, and Wilkins 2008.

References

Aboud, F. (1988) *Children and Prejudice*. Basil Blackwell.
Adams, N. and Bettis, P. (2003) "Commanding the Room in Short Skirts: Cheering as the Embodiment of Ideal Girlhood," *Gender and Society* 17(1): 73–91.
Adler, P. A. and Adler, P. (1998) *Peer Power*. Rutgers University Press.
Adler, P. A., Kless, S. J., and Adler, P. (1992) "Socialization to Gender Roles: Popularity among Elementary School Boys and Girls," *Sociology of Education* 65(3): 169–87.
Alpes, M. J. and Spire, A. (2014) "Dealing with Law in Migration Control: The Powers of Street-Level Bureaucrats at French Consulates," *Social & Legal Studies* 23(2): 261–74.
Armstrong, E. and Hamilton, L. (2013) *Paying for the Party: How College Maintains Inequality*. Harvard University Press.
Augustine, J., Cavanagh, S., and Crosnoe, R. (2009) "Maternal Education, Early Childcare and the Reproduction of Advantage," *Social Forces* 88(1): 1–29.
Authier, Y.-A. and Lehman-Frisch, S. (2015) "Social Diversity in Gentrified Neighborhoods: Child's Play?," translated by C. Mitrakos. *Metropolitics*, December 4, 2015, https://metropolitiques.eu/Social-Diversity-in-Gentrified.html
Auyero, J. and Benzecry, C. (2017) "The Practical Logic of Political Domination: Conceptualizing the Clientelist Habitus," *Sociological Theory* 35(3): 179–99.
Bargel, L. and Darmon, M. (2017) "Political Socialization," *Politika. Encyclopédie des Sciences Historiques et Sociales du Politique*, https://www.politika.io/en/notice/political-socialisation

References

Becker, H. (1963) *Outsiders: Studies in the Sociology of Deviance*. The Free Press.
Becker, H. (1970) "The Self and Adult Socialization." In: *Sociological Work: Method and Substance*, 289–303. Transaction Books.
Becker, H., Geer, B., Hughes, E., and Strauss, A. (1992) *Boys in White: Student Culture in Medical School*. Transaction Publishers.
Berger, P. and Kellner, H. (1964) "Marriage and the Construction of Reality," *Diogenes* 46: 1–23.
Berger, P. and Luckmann, T. (1991) *The Social Construction of Reality: A Treatise in the Sociology of Knowledge*, 6th edition. Penguin Books.
Bernstein, B. (2003) *Class, Codes and Control. Vol. I. Theoretical Studies towards a Sociology of Language*. Routledge.
Bernstein, B. and Young, D. (1967) "Social Class Differences in Conceptions of the Uses of Toys," *Sociology* 1(2): 131–40.
Bertrand, J. (2011) "Vocation at the Intersection of Different Socialization Spaces: A Sociological Study of Professional Soccer Players' Training in France," *Sociétés contemporaines* 82: 85–106.
Bertrand, J., Court, M., Mennesson, C., and Zabban, V. (2015) "Male Socializations: From Childhood to Adulthood," *Terrains & travaux* 27(2), https://www.cairn-int.info/journal-terrains-et-travaux-2015-2-page-5.htm
Bettie, J. (2003) *Women without Class: Girls, Race and Identity*. University of California Press.
Boltanski, L. (1971) "Les usages sociaux du corps," *Annales. Histoire, Sciences Sociales* 26(1): 205–33.
Bourdieu, P. (1977) *Outline of a Theory of Practice*. Translated by R. Nice. Cambridge University Press.
Bourdieu, P. (1984) *Distinction: A Social Critique of the Judgement of Taste*. Translated by R. Nice. Harvard University Press.
Bourdieu, P. (1986) "The Forms of Capital." In: Richardson, J. (ed.) *Handbook of Theory and Research for the Sociology of Education*, 16–29. Greenwood Press.
Bourdieu, P. (1990) *The Logic of Practice*. Translated by R. Nice. Polity.
Bourdieu, P. (1998) *Practical Reason: On the Theory of Action*. Translated by R. Johnson et al. Polity.
Bourdieu, P. (2000) *Pascalian Meditations*. Translated by R. Nice. Polity.
Bourdieu, P. and Passeron, J.-C. (1979) *The Inheritors: French Students and Their Relation to Culture*. Translated by R. Nice. University of Chicago Press.

Bourdieu, P. and Passeron, J.-C. (1990) *Reproduction in Education, Society and Culture.* Translated by R. Nice. Sage Publications.

Bourgois, P. and Schonberg, J. (2007) "Ethnic Dimensions of Habitus among Homeless Heroin Injectors," *Ethnography* 8(1): 7–31.

Bronfenbrenner, U. (1966) "Socialization and Social Class through Time and Space." In: Bendix, R. and Lipset, S. M. (eds.) *Class, Status and Power*, 362–77. The Free Press.

Brown-Saracino, J. (2018) *How Places Make Us: Novel LBQ Identities in Four Small Cities.* University of Chicago Press.

Cahill, S. E. (1999) "Emotional Capital and Professional Socialization: The Case of Mortuary Science Students (and Me)," *Social Psychology Quarterly* 62(2): 101–16.

Calarco, J. M. C. (2018) *Negotiating Opportunities: How the Middle Class Secures Advantages in School.* Oxford University Press.

Cartier, M., Coutant, I., Masclet, O., and Siblot, Y. (2016) *The France of the Little-Middles: A Suburban Housing Development in Greater Paris.* Translated by J. Rodgers. Berghahn Books.

Cayouette-Remblière, J., Lion, G., and Rivière, C. (2019) "Socialisations par l'espace, socialisations à l'espace. Les dimensions spatiales de la (trans)formation des individus," *Sociétés contemporaines* 115(3): 5–31.

Cerulo, K. (2018) "Scents and Sensibility: Olfaction, Sense-Making, and Meaning Attribution," *American Sociological Review* 83(2): 361–89.

Chamboredon, J.-C. (2015) "La délinquance juvénile, essai de construction d'objet." In: Chamboredon, J.-C. *Jeunesse et classes sociales*, 87–129. Presses de l'ENS.

Chamboredon, J.-C. and Prévot, J. (1975) "Changes in the Social Definition of Early Childhood and the New Forms of Symbolic Violence," *Theory and Society* 2(3): 331–50.

Chamboredon, J.-C. and Prévot, J. (2015) "Le 'métier d'enfant.'" In: Chamboredon, J.-C. *Jeunesse et classes sociales*, 131–74. Presses de l'ENS.

Chapoulie, J.-M. (2020) *Chicago Sociology.* Translated by C. Walzer. Columbia University Press.

Cheng, S. H. and Kuo, W. H. (2000) "Family Socialization of Ethnic Identity among Chinese American Pre-Adolescents," *Journal of Comparative Family Studies* 31(4): 463–84.

Chin, T. and Phillips, M. (2004) "Social Reproduction and Child-Rearing Practices: Social Class, Children's Agency, and the Summer Activity Gap," *Sociology of Education* 77(3): 185–210.

Condry, J. and Condry, S. (1976) "Sex Differences: A Study of the Eye of the Beholder," *Child Development* 47(3): 812–19.
Connell, R. W. (1985) "Theorising Gender," *Sociology* 19(2): 260–72.
Connell, R. W. (2005) *Masculinities*, 2nd edition. University of California Press.
Connell, R. W. (2012) "Gender, Health and Theory: Conceptualizing the Issue, in Local and World Perspective," *Social Science and Medicine* 74(11): 1675–83.
Connell, R. W. and Messerschmidt, J. W. (2005) "Hegemonic Masculinity: Rethinking the Concept," *Gender and Society* 19(6): 829–59.
Connolly, P., Kelly, B., and Smith, A. (2009) "Ethnic Habitus and Young Children: A Case Study of Northern Ireland," *European Early Childhood Education Research Journal* 17(2): 217–32.
Cookson, P. W. and Persell, C. H. (1985) *Preparing for Power: America's Elite Boarding Schools*. Basic Books.
Corsaro, W. A. (1992) "Interpretive Reproduction in Children's Peer Cultures," *Social Psychology Quarterly* 55(2): 160–77.
Corsaro, W. A. and Eder, D. (1990) "Children's Peer Cultures," *Annual Review of Sociology* 16: 197–220.
Darmon, M. (2012) "A People Thinning Institution: Changing Bodies and Souls in a Commercial Weight-Loss Group," *Ethnography* 13(3): 379–402.
Darmon, M. (2013) *Classes préparatoires. La fabrique d'une jeunesse dominante*. La Découverte.
Darmon, M. (2017) *Becoming Anorexic: A Sociological Study*. Translated by L. Garnier. Routledge.
Darmon, M. (2018) "Drafting the 'Time Space.' Attitudes towards Time among Prep School Students," *European Societies* 20(3): 525–48.
Darmon, M. (2020) "The School Form of the Hospital: How Does Social Class Affect Post-Stroke Patients in Rehabilitation Units?," *Qualitative Sociology* 43: 235–54.
Darmon, M. (2021) *Réparer les cerveaux. Sociologie des pertes et des récupérations post-AVC*. La Découverte.
Darmon, M., Dulong D., and Favier, E. (2019) "Time and Power," *Actes de la Recherche en Sciences Sociales* 226–27: 6–15.
Davis, F. (1968) "Professional Socialization as Subjective Experience: The Process of Doctrinal Conversion among Student Nurses." In: Becker, H., Greer, B., Riesman, D., and Weiss, R. (eds.) *Institutions and the Person. Festschrift in Honor of Everett C. Hughes*, 235–51. Aldine.
Defoe, D. (2007) *Robinson Crusoe*. Oxford University Press.

Desmond, M. (2006) "Becoming a Firefighter," *Ethnography* 7(4): 387–421.
DiMaggio, P. (1997) "Culture and Cognition," *Annual Review of Sociology* 23: 263–87.
DiMaggio, P. and Garip, F. (2012) "Network Effects and Social Inequality," *Annual Review of Sociology* 38: 93–118.
Douglas, M. (1986) *How Institutions Think*. Syracuse University Press.
Dubar, C. (2004) *La Socialisation*. 3rd edition. Armand Colin.
Dubois, V. (2010) *The Bureaucrat and the Poor: Encounters in French Welfare Offices*. Translated by J.-Y. Bart. Routledge.
Durkheim, E. (1956) *Education and Sociology*. Translated by S. D. Fox. The Free Press.
Durkheim, E. (1977) *Selected Writings on Education. Vol. II. The Evolution of Educational Thought*. Translated by P. Collins. Routledge.
Durkheim, E. (1995) *The Elementary Forms of Religious Life*. Translated by K. E. Fields. The Free Press.
Durkheim, E. (2005) *Suicide: A Study in Sociology*. Translated by J. A. Spaulding and G. Simpson. Routledge.
Elias, N. (1991) *The Society of Individuals*. Translated by E. Jephcott. Basil Blackwell.
Elias, N. (1993) *Mozart: Portrait of a Genius*. Translated by E. Jephcott. Polity.
Elias, N. (1994) *The Civilizing Process: Sociogenetic and Psychogenetic Investigations*. Translated by E. Jephcott. Blackwell.
Ferguson, A. A. (2000) *Bad Boys: Public Schools in the Making of Black Masculinity*. University of Michigan Press.
Fillieule, O. (2010) "Some Elements of an Interactionist Approach to Political Disengagement," *Social Movement Studies* 9(1): 1–15.
Fillieule, O. (2013) "Political Socialization and Social Movements." In: Snow, D. A., Della Porta, D., Klandermans, B., and McAdam, D. (eds.) *The Wiley-Blackwell Encyclopedia of Social and Political Movements*, 968–74. Wiley-Blackwell.
Fillieule, O. and Neveu, E. (eds.) (2019) *Activists Forever? Long-Term Impacts of Political Activism*. Cambridge University Press.
Fine, G. A. (1987) *With the Boys: Little League Baseball and Preadolescent Culture*. University of Chicago Press.
Foucault, M. (1995) *Discipline and Punish: The Birth of the Prison*. Translated by A. Sheridan. Vintage Books.
Gansen, H. M. (2017) "Reproducing (and Disrupting) Heteronormativity: Gendered Sexual Socialization in Preschool Classrooms," *Sociology of Education* 90(3): 255–72.

References

Garces, C. and Jones, A. (2009) "Mauss Redux: From Warfare's Human Toll to L'homme total," *Anthropological Quarterly* 82(1): 279–309.

Garfinkel, H. (1967) *Studies in Ethnomethodology*. Prentice-Hall.

Garner, B. and Grazian, D. (2016) "Naturalizing Gender through Childhood Socialization Messages in a Zoo," *Social Psychology Quarterly* 79(3): 181–98.

Gianini Belotti, E. (1999) *Dalla parte delle bambine. L'influenza dei condizionamenti sociali nella formazione del ruolo femminile nei primi anni di vita*. Feltrinelli.

Goffman, E. (1961) *Asylums: Essays on the Social Situation of Mental Patients and Other Inmates*. Anchor Books.

Goffman, E. (1977) "The Arrangement between the Sexes," *Theory and Society* 4(3): 301–31.

Gojard, S. (2010) *Le Métier de mère*. La Dispute.

Graham, L. O. (1999) *Our Kind of People: Inside America's Black Upper Class*. HarperCollins.

Grant, J. (2013) "Parent–Child Relations in Western Europe and North America, 1500–Present." In: Fass, P. S. (ed.) *The Routledge History of Childhood in the Western World*, 103–24. Routledge.

Green, A. I. (2008) "Erotic Habitus: Toward a Sociology of Desire," *Theory and Society* 37(6): 597–626.

Gregory, E. (2001) "Sisters and Brothers as Language and Literacy Teachers: Synergy between Siblings Playing and Working Together," *Journal of Early Childhood Literacy* 1(3): 301–22.

Guhin, J., McCrory Calarco, J., and Miller-Idriss, C. (2021) "Whatever Happened to Socialization?," *Annual Review of Sociology* 47(1): 109–29.

Gutman, M. (2013) "The Physical Spaces of Childhood." In: Fass, P. S. (ed.) *The Routledge History of Childhood in the Western World*, 249–66. Routledge.

Haegel, F. (2020) "Political Socialisation: Out of Purgatory?" *European Journal of Sociology* 61(3): 333–64.

Hagerman, M. (2014) "White Families and Race: Colour-Blind and Colour-Conscious Approaches to White Racial Socialization," *Ethnic and Racial Studies* 37(14): 2598–614.

Hagerman, M. (2016) "White Racial Socialization: Progressive Fathers on Raising 'Antiracist' Children," *Journal of Marriage and Family* 79(1): 60–74.

Hagerman, M. (2018) *White Kids: Growing Up with Privilege in a Racially Divided America*. New York University Press.

Harvey, P. F. (2022) "'Make Sure You Look Someone in the Eye':

Socialization and Classed Comportment in Two Elementary Schools," *American Journal of Sociology* 127(5): 1417–59.

Hasenfeld, Y. (1972) "People Processing Organizations: An Exchange Approach," *American Sociological Review* 37(3): 256–63.

Heyl, B. S. (1977) "The Madam as Teacher: The Training of House Prostitutes," *Social Problems* 24(5): 545–55.

Hochschild, A. R. (1979) "Emotion Work, Feeling Rules, and Social Structure," *American Journal of Sociology* 85(3): 551–75.

Hochschild, A. R. (2012) *The Managed Heart: Commercialization of Human Feeling. Updated with a New Preface.* University of California Press.

Hoggart, R. (1971) *The Uses of Literacy: Aspects of Working-Class Life, with Special Reference to Publications and Entertainments.* Chatto and Windus.

Hoggart, R. (1989) *Life and Times: A Local Habitation, 1918–40.* Oxford University Press.

Holloway, S. L. and Valentine, G. (2000) "Spatiality and the New Social Studies of Childhood," *Sociology* 34(4): 763–83.

Hughes, E. C. (1956) "The Making of a Physician – General Statement of Ideas and Problems," *Human Organization* 14(4): 21–5.

Hugues, D., Rodriguez, J., Smith, E. P., Johnson, D. J., Stevenson, H. C., and Spicer, P. (2006) "Parents' Ethnic-Racial Socialization Practices: A Review of Research and Directions for Future Study," *Developmental Psychology* 42(5): 747–70.

James, A. (2013) *Socialising Children.* Palgrave Macmillan.

Jenkins, T. M., Underman, K., Vinson, A. H., Olsen, L. D., and Hirshfield L. E. (2021) "The Resurgence of Medical Education in Sociology: A Return to Our Roots and an Agenda for the Future," *Journal of Health and Social Behavior* 62(3): 255–70.

Kane, E. (2006) "'No Way My Boys Are Going to Be Like That!': Parents' Responses to Children's Gender Nonconformity," *Gender & Society* 20(2): 149–76.

Khan, S. R. (2011) *Privilege: The Making of an Adolescent Elite at St. Paul's School.* Princeton University Press.

Kosunen, S. and Rivière, C. (2018) "Alone or Together in the Neighbourhood? School Choice and Families' Access to Local Social Networks," *Children's Geographies* 16(2): 143–55.

Kusserow, A. S. (2004) *American Individualisms: Child Rearing and Social Class in Three Neighborhoods.* Palgrave Macmillan.

Lahire, B. (1999) "De la théorie de l'habitus à une sociologie psychologique." In: *Le Travail sociologique de Pierre Bourdieu.* La Découverte.

Lahire, B. (2002) *Portraits sociologiques*. Nathan.
Lahire, B. (2004) *La Culture des individus. Dissonances culturelles et distinction de soi*. La Découverte.
Lahire, B. (2005) *L'Esprit sociologique*. La Découverte.
Lahire, B. (2011) *The Plural Actor*. Translated by D. Fernbach. Polity.
Lahire, B. (2012a) *Monde Pluriel*. Seuil.
Lahire, B. (2012b) *Tableaux de familles. Heurs et malheurs scolaires en milieux populaires*. Seuil/Gallimard.
Lahire, B. (2013) *Dans les plis singuliers du social*. La Découverte.
Lahire, B. (ed.) (2019) *Enfances de classe. De l'inégalité parmi les enfants*. Seuil.
Lahire, B. (2020) *The Sociological Interpretation of Dreams*. Translated by H. Morrison. Polity.
Lareau, A. (2002) "Invisible Inequality: Social Class and Childrearing in Black Families and White Families," *American Sociological Review* 67: 747–76.
Lareau, A. (2011) *Unequal Childhoods: Class, Race and Family Life. Second Edition with an Update a Decade Later*. University of California Press.
Lareau, A. and Calarco, J. M. (2012) "Class, Cultural Capital, and Institutions: The Case of Families and Schools." In: Fiske, S. T. and Markus, H. R. (eds.) *Facing Social Class: How Societal Rank Influences Interaction*, 61–86. Russell Sage Foundation.
Levi Martin, J. (2000) "What Do Animals Do All Day?: The Division of Labor, Class Bodies, and Totemic Thinking in the Popular Imagination," *Poetics* 27(2–3): 195–231.
Li, S. and Seale, C. (2008) "Acquiring a Sociological Identity: An Observational Study of a PhD Project," *Sociology* 42(5): 987–1002.
Lignier, W. (2020) "Words Also Make Us: Enhancing the Sociology of Embodiment with Cultural Psychology," *European Journal of Social Theory* 23(1): 15–32.
Lignier, W. (2021a) "The Discovery of Symbolic Violence: How Toddlers Learn to Prevail with Words," *Ethnography* 22(2): 246–66.
Lignier, W. (2021b) "Symbolic Power for Beginners: The Very First Social Efforts to Control Others' Actions and Perceptions," *Sociological Theory* 39(4): 201–24.
Lignier, W. and Pagis, J. (2012) "Children Articulating Social Order: A Study on Children's Classifications and Judgments," *Politix* 99(3): 23–49.
Lignier, W. and Pagis, J. (2017a) *L'Enfance de l'ordre. Comment les enfants perçoivent le monde social*. Seuil.

Lignier, W. and Pagis, J. (2017b) "'Left' vs. 'Right': How French Children Reconstruct the Political Field," *American Behavioral Scientist* 61(2): 167–85.

Linhart, R. (1981) *The Assembly Line*. Translated by M. Crosland. University of Massachusetts Press.

McAdam, D. (1988) *Freedom Summer*. Oxford University Press.

Maghbouleh, N. (2017) *The Limits of Whiteness: Iranian Americans and the Everyday Politics of Race*. Stanford University Press.

Mannheim, K. (1952) "The Problem of Generations." In: Kecskemet, P. (ed.) *Essays*, 276–322. Routledge.

Martin, C. (2023) "Educating Parents: Critical Policy Issues." In: Daly, M., Gilbert N., Pfau-Effinger B., and Besharov D. (eds.) *International Handbook of Family Policy: A Life-Course Perspective*, 633–650. Oxford University Press.

Martin, K. A. (1998) "Becoming a Gendered Body: Practices of Preschools," *American Sociological Review* 63(4): 494–511.

Martin, K. A. and Luke, K. (2010) "Gender Differences in the ABC's of the Birds and the Bees: What Mothers Teach Young Children about Sexuality and Reproduction," *Sex Roles* 62: 278–91.

Masclet, C. (2015) "Inherited Feminism: Children of Second-Wave Feminist Activists," *Politix* 109: 45–68, https://www.cairn-int.info/journal--2015-1-page-45.htm

Mauss, M. (1973) "Techniques of the Body," *Economy and Society* 2: 70–88.

Mead, G. H. (1934) *Mind, Self, and Society*. University of Chicago Press.

Mears, A. (2011) *Pricing Beauty: The Making of a Fashion Model*. University of California Press.

Mennesson, C., Bertrand, J., and Court, M. (2019) "Boys Who Don't Like Sports: Family Lifestyle and Transmission of Dispositions," *Sport, Education and Society* 24(3): 269–82.

Merton, R. K., Reader, G. G., and Kendall, P. L. (eds.) (1957) *The Student-Physician: Introductory Studies in the Sociology of Medical Education*. Harvard University Press.

Merton, R. K. and Rossi, A. S. (1968) "Contributions to the Theory of Reference Group Behavior." In: Merton, R. K. *Social Theory and Social Structure*, 279–334. The Free Press.

Messner, M. (1992) *Power at Play: Sports and the Problem of Masculinity*. Beacon Press.

Millet, M. and Thin, D. (2005) "Le temps des familles populaires à l'épreuve de la précarité," *Lien social et politiques* 54: 153–62.

Morris, E. W. (2005) "'Tuck in That Shirt!' Race, Class, Gender and Discipline in an Urban School," *Sociological Perspectives* 48(1): 25–48.

Morris, E. W. (2008) "Rednecks, Rutters, and Rithmetics: Social Class, Masculinity, and Schooling in a Rural Context," *Gender and Society* 22(6): 728–51.

Musto, M. (2019) "Brilliant or Bad: The Gendered Social Construction of Exceptionalism in Early Adolescence," *American Sociological Review* 84(3): 369–93.

Noiriel, G. (2003) "Un concept opératoire: 'l'habitus national' dans la sociologie de Norbert Elias." In: *Penser avec, penser contre*, 171–88. Belin.

Pagis, J. (2018) *May '68: Shaping Political Generations*. Translated by K. Throssell. Amsterdam University Press.

Parsons, T. and Bales, R. (1955) *Family, Socialization and Interaction Process*. The Free Press.

Pollak, L. H. and Thoits, P. A. (1989) "Processes in Emotional Socialization," *Social Psychology Quarterly* 52(1): 22–34.

Priest, N., Walton, J., White, F., Kowal, E., Baker, A., and Paradies, Y. (2014) "Understanding the Complexities of Ethnic-Racial Socialization Processes for Both Minority and Majority Groups: A 30-Year Systematic Review," *International Journal of Intercultural Relations* 43: 139–55.

Prot, S., Anderson, C. A., Gentile, D. A., Warburton, W., Saleem, M., Groves, C. L., and Brown, S. C. (2015) "Media as Agents of Socialization." In: Grusec, J. E. and Hastings, P. D. (eds.) *Handbook of Socialization*, 2nd edition, 276–300. Guilford Press.

Rivière, C. (2012) "Children's Autonomy and Our Relationship with Public Spaces." Translated by O. Waine. *Metropolitics*, November 7, https://metropolitics.org/Children-s-autonomy-and-our.html

Rubin, J. Z., Provenzano, F. J., and Luria, Z. (1974) "The Eye of the Beholder: Parents' Views on Sex of Newborns," *American Journal of Orthopsychiatry* 44(4): 512–19.

Sallaz, J. J. (2010) "Talking Race, Marketing Culture: The Racial Habitus In and Out of Apartheid," *Social Problems* 57(2): 294–314.

Samuel, O., Brachet, S., Brugeilles, C., Paillet, A., Pélage, A., and Rollet, C. (2014) "Préparer la naissance: une affaire de genre," *Politiques sociales et familiales* 116: 5–14.

Sawicki, F. and Siméant, J. (2010) "Decompartmentalizing the Sociology of Activist Commitment. A Critical Survey of Some Recent Trends in French Research," *Sociologie du travail* 52: e83–e109.

Schilt, K., (2006) "Just One of the Guys? How Transmen Make Gender Visible at Work," *Gender and Society* 20(4): 465–90.

References

Schleef, D. J. (2006) *Managing Elites: Professional Socialization in Law and Business Schools*. Rowman and Littlefield.

Schmidt, J. (2013) "Children and the State." In: Fass, P. S. (ed.) *The Routledge History of Childhood in the Western World*, 174–90. Routledge.

Seron, C., Silbey, S., Cech, E., and Rubineau, B. (2015) "Persistence Is Cultural: Professional Socialization and the Reproduction of Sex Segregation," *Work and Occupations* 43(2): 178–214.

Sigel, R. S. (ed.) (1989) *Political Learning in Adulthood: A Sourcebook of Theory and Research*. University of Chicago Press.

Siméant, J. (2013) "Committing to Internationalisation: Careers of African Participants at the World Social Forum," *Social Movement Studies: Journal of Social, Cultural and Political Protest* 12(3): 245–63.

Simmel, G. (1950) *The Sociology of Georg Simmel*. Translated by K. H. Wolff. The Free Press.

Singh-Manoux, A. and Marmot, M. (2005) "The Role of Socialization in Explaining Social Inequalities in Health," *Social Science and Medicine* 60(9): 2129–33.

Small, M. L., Harding, D. J., and Lamont, M. (2010) "Reconsidering Culture and Poverty," *The ANNALS of the American Academy of Political and Social Science* 629 (1): 6–27.

Stoker, L. and Jennings, M. K. (1995) "Life-Cycle Transitions and Political Participation: The Case of Marriage," *The American Political Science Review* 89(2): 421–33.

Strauss, A. (1977) *Mirrors and Masks: The Search for Identity*. Martin Robinson.

Streib, J. (2015) *The Power of The Past: Understanding Cross-Class Marriages*. Oxford University Press.

Streib, J. (2020) *Privilege Lost: Who Leaves the Upper Middle Class and How They Fall*. Oxford University Press.

Travisano, R. (1970) "Alternation and Conversion as Qualitatively Different Transformations." In: Stone, G. P. and Farberman, H. A. (eds.) *Social Psychology through Symbolic Interaction*, 237–48. Ginn-Blaisdell.

Van Ausdale, D. and Feagin, J. R. (1996) "Using Racial and Ethnic Concepts: The Critical Case of Very Young Children," *American Sociological Review* 61(5): 779–93.

Vandebroeck, D. (2017) *Distinctions in the Flesh: Social Class and the Embodiment of Inequality*. Routledge.

Vincent, C., Rollock, N., Ball, S., and Gillborn, D. (2013) "Raising Middle-Class Black Children: Parenting Priorities, Actions and Strategies," *Sociology* 47(3): 427–42.

Vincent, G., Lahire, B., and Thin, D. (1994) "Sur l'histoire et la théorie de la forme scolaire." In: Vincent, G. (ed.) *L'Éducation prisonnière de la forme scolaire?*, 11–48. PUL.

Wacquant, L. (1995) "Pugs at Work: Bodily Capital and Bodily Labour among Professional Boxers," *Body and Society* 1(1): 65–93.

Wacquant, L. (2003) *Body and Soul: Notebooks of an Apprentice Boxer*. Oxford University Press.

Wacquant, L. (2022) "Resolving the Trouble with 'Race,'" *New Left Review* 133/4: 67–88.

Wagner, A.-C. (2020) "The Internationalization of Elite Education." In: Denord, F. et al. (eds.) *Researching Elites and Power: Theory, Methods, Analyses*, 193–202. Springer.

Weininger, E., Lareau, A., and LaRossa, R. (2009) "Paradoxical Pathways: An Ethnographic Extension of Kohn's Findings on Class and Childrearing," *Journal of Marriage and Family* 71(3): 680–95.

West, C. and Fenstermaker, S. (1995) "Doing Difference," *Gender and Society* 9(1): 8–37.

West, C. and Zimmerman, D. H. (1987) "Doing Gender," *Gender and Society* 1(2): 125–51.

Wilkins, A. (2008) *Wannabes, Goths, and Christians: The Boundaries of Sex, Style and Status*. University of Chicago Press.

Williams, A. J., Vernon, J. A., Williams, M. C., and Malecha, K. (1987) "Sex Role Socialization in Picture Books: An Update," *Social Science Quarterly* 68(1): 148–56.

Winchester, D. and Guhin, J. (2019) "Praying 'Straight from the Heart': Evangelical Sincerity and the Normative Frames of Culture in Action," *Poetics* 72: 32–42.

Winkler, E. (2011) "'My Aunt Talks about Black People All the Time': The Significance of Extended Family Networks in the Racial Socialization of African American Adolescents." In: Aborampah, O-M. and Sudarkasa, N. (eds.) *Extended Families in Africa and the African Diaspora*, 273–95. Africa World Press.

Winkler, E. (2012) *Learning Race, Learning Place: Shaping Racial Identities and Ideas in African American Childhoods*. Rutgers University Press.

Wood, E., Desmarais, S., and Gugula, S. (2002) "The Impact of Parenting Experience on Gender Stereotyped Toy Play of Children," *Sex Roles* 47: 39–49.

Wrong, D. (1961) "The Oversocialized Conception of Man in Modern Sociology," *American Sociological Review* 26(2): 183–93.

Zelizer, V. (1985) *Pricing the Priceless Child: The Changing Social Value of Children*. Basic Books.

Zerubavel, E. (1981) *Hidden Rhythms: Schedule and Calendars in Social Life*. University of Chicago Press.

Zerubavel, E. (1997) *Social Mindscapes: An Invitation to Cognitive Sociology*. Harvard University Press.

Index

Aboud, F. 142, 150
age 64, 106, 115, 120, 135, 166–7
  see also life course
agency 4, 6, 7, 138, 163–9
alternation 131, 174–5 n.6
anticipatory socialization 86–7
Armstrong, E. and Hamilton, L. 121
authority 11, 13, 30–2, 41–2, 165–6
Auyero, J. and Benzecry, C. 103, 112

Becker, H. 88–95, 102, 109–11
  see also Boys in White
Berger, P. 174 n.6
  and Kellner, H. 99, 117
  and Luckmann, T. 8, 11–12, 60, 78–83, 88, 117–18, 120, 131
  see also Social Construction of Reality
Bernstein, B. 25–6, 32–3
biology 21, 36, 47, 49, 51, 171

body 4, 15–18, 26, 45–6, 50, 58, 73, 108, 115, 117–20, 144–8, 151, 174 n.1
Boltanski, L. 43–4, 128
books 17, 20, 25, 59, 65, 119, 127
Bourdieu, P. 6, 8–9, 14–23, 26–7, 38, 42–3, 45, 67, 112, 120, 123, 126, 128, 130–1, 148, 153–4, 157, 159–61, 163, 174 n.1, 175 n.9
  and Passeron, J.-C. 17, 20, 128, 130
  see also cultural capital, disposition(s), *Distinction*, habitus, hysteresis, *Logic of Practice (The)*, *Reproduction*
Bourgois, P. and Schonberg, J. 146–8, 153
Boys in White 88–95
Brown-Saracino, J. 101–2

Cahill S. E. 97, 125–6
Calarco, J. 43, 71

capital
  cultural 17, 21–2, 31, 33, 38, 43, 59, 133, 161
  economic 21–2, 43, 161
  school 21, 74
  social 21, 40, 102
Chamboredon, J.-C. 6, 32–3, 69, 75
childcare 54, 63–4, 66, 75, 100, 107
children 8–81, 99, 118–19, 124, 127, 134, 136–43, 149–50, 161–8
class 1, 7, 19–23, 25–44, 48, 51, 54, 60–5, 68, 70–6, 92, 100, 111–12, 115, 121, 124, 128, 144–6, 153, 157, 161, 165
  middle class 48, 51, 61–2, 64–5, 75, 124–5, 142–3, 165, 167
  upper class 54, 68, 72, 140–1, 150
  working class 54, 60–1, 63–5, 70–3, 75, 111–12, 124, 133, 140, 145–7
clothing 45–6, 49, 72–3, 81, 115, 146–7
cognition 17, 65–6, 74, 116, 126–8, 142, 163
Connell, R. W. 155, 158–61, 174 n.1
Connolly, P. 142, 149–50
conversion 81, 88, 96, 128, 130–5, 174–5 n.6
Cookson, P. W. and Persell, C. H. 4, 72
criticism(s) of socialization 6–7, 13, 155–60, 163–4, 168–9, 170–3
culture 10, 17, 25, 59, 61, 73, 93, 98, 101–2, 111, 128–9, 139, 149, 153, 159
  childhood culture 164, 168

class culture 31, 38–9
medical culture 84–8
peer culture 67–8, 168
student culture 88, 110

Darmon, M. 37–9, 74, 102–3, 115, 119, 133, 175 n.8
Davis, F. 96
Desmond, M. 97, 112
determinism 6–7, 68, 107, 163–6, 171–2
DiMaggio, P. 67, 102
dispositions 7, 14, 18, 34–5, 56–9, 62–3, 66–7, 98, 102–4, 123, 130–3, 167–8
  class dispositions 20–1, 28–9, 39–40, 71, 74–5, 100, 133
  emotional dispositions 126
  gender dispositions 45, 50–1, 121–2, 129, 156–62
  and predispositions 111–14
  and race 136–7, 140, 144–9, 152–3
Distinction 22, 26–7
domination 20, 119, 140, 153–5, 159–61, 167–8
  see also inequality, intersectionality, reproduction
dreams 57–8, 91
drugs 102, 146–8
Durkheim, E. 3, 8–14, 18, 20, 23–4, 34, 36, 65, 81, 86, 113, 123, 130–1, 148, 170–2
  See also *Education and Sociology*

Education and Sociology 3, 9–14
educational norms 12–13, 54–5, 63–7, 165
Elias, N. 1, 8, 24–5, 54

embodiment 153, 155, 158, 174 n.1, 175 n.9
  see also incorporation
emotion(s) 28–9, 45, 47, 75, 79–82, 100, 123–6
ethnicity *see* race
ethnic-racial socialization *see* race

Ferguson, A. Arnett 40–2, 140
Fillieule, O. 7, 103–4
food 2, 25–7, 39, 47, 79, 103, 115, 127
Foucault, M. 108, 117
friends 30, 40, 95, 99, 100, 112, 115, 117, 143, 147
  see also peers

Garfinkel, H. 129
gender 29, 44–51, 60, 70, 72–3, 93–4, 100, 115, 117, 119, 124–5, 128–30, 155–63, 166–8, 175 n.10
  doing gender 155–61
  performance 160, 175 n.10
  transgender people 101, 121–2, 129
  see also disposition, embodiment, incorporation, intersectionality
Gianini Belotti, E. 46–7
Goffman, E. 49, 60, 108–9, 111, 132
Graham, L. Otis 40–1, 141, 150
Guhin, J. 7, 10, 102, 138

habitus 14–23, 61–2, 67, 98, 103–4, 111–13, 118, 120, 123, 126, 128–30
  and class 21–2, 28
  and gender 45–6, 51, 153, 156
  Lahire's criticism of 56–8
  and race 144–5
Hagerman, M. A. 138, 142–3
Hasenfeld, Y., 109
health 26, 43–4, 65, 74, 119–20, 160
hegemonic masculinity 155, 158–61
history 18–19, 23–5, 53–5, 148, 171
Hochschild, A. R. 82, 123–5
Hoggart, R. 27, 38–9
hospital(s) 74, 84–5, 89, 95, 108–10, 115, 134
Hughes, E. C. 84, 87–9, 93, 96
Hugues, D. 137–9
hysteresis 19–20, 129, 131–2

identity 101, 114, 121, 137–9, 143, 145, 168
incorporation 14–18, 21, 45–6, 145, 149–52, 159–60, 171, 174 n.1, 175 n.9
inequality(ies) 51, 20, 26, 43–4, 51, 70, 74, 102, 167, 173
institution(s) 53–6, 65, 69, 73–4, 80–2, 86, 88, 90, 95, 98–9, 104, 115–17, 119–20, 132–3, 156
  class dispositions and institutions 30–1, 41–3
  as socializing agents 108–13, 121, 129–30
  see also school
intersectionality 7, 51, 73, 115, 140–6, 153–5, 157, 160–2, 166–8, 175 n.10

Khan, S. 72–3

Lahire, B. 6, 23, 36, 55–61, 68–71, 76, 99–100, 112, 117–18, 123, 133
  See also Plural Actor (The)

language 16, 30, 35, 70–1, 82–3, 117–19, 139
Lareau, A. 29–32, 36–7, 43, 71, 75, 142, 165
leisure 27, 29–37, 47–51, 142, 164
life course 6, 75, 80, 106–7, 120–2, 129, 134–5
Lignier, W. 118, 166–7
Logic of Practice (The) 14–23

McAdam, D. 113–14
Maghbouleh, N. 150–1
Mannheim, K. 24
marital socialization 79, 99–100, 116–17, 134
Martin, K. 70, 162
Mauss, M. 16, 45, 123
Mead, G. H. 78–9, 87, 90
media 65, 67, 75–6, 100, 151–2, 162
Merton, R. K. 84–7, 89
  See also Student-Physician (The)
money 28–9, 38–9, 41–2, 62, 100, 114, 121, 147, 153
Morris, E. 72–3, 175 n.10
music 17, 24, 37, 49, 72, 82, 114
Musto, M. 70, 145–6

nature 18, 19, 27, 51, 152–3
neighborhood 34–5, 40–1, 75, 101, 151
  see also space

objects 15, 34, 47, 59, 71, 127, 163, 167
occupational socialization *see* professional socialization

Pagis, J. 114, 166
parents
  as agents of primary socialization 8–52, 68, 75, 124, 137–43, 150–2, 164–6
  as heterogeneous agents of primary socialization 60–3
  as socialized subjects 64–6, 100
Parsons, T. 10, 44–6, 50, 86
partners *see* marital socialization
peers 54–5, 65, 66–9, 85, 162, 164, 166
play 30–4, 40, 47–51, 58, 68, 141, 164–5
  see also sport, leisure
Plural Actor (The) 23, 30–1, 56–8, 118
political socialization *see* politics
politics 22, 95, 99–100, 101–4, 113–14, 131
prison 97, 108–110, 147
professional socialization 80–98, 103, 117, 121–2, 125–9, 134–5

race 39–42, 44, 51, 72–3, 136–55, 160–1, 168, 175 n.10
racial socialization *see* race
religion 56, 102, 104, 130–1, 149, 174 n.6
reproduction 7, 10, 13, 49, 102, 128–30
Reproduction 20, 128–31

Schilt, K. 121–2
school 65–6, 93–4, 97, 100, 113, 129–30, 134, 143, 150–1
  as an agent of socialization 69–76, 119, 145–6
  and class dispositions 32–3, 36–7, 41–3, 59–61, 133

college and higher education 83–4, 84–93, 121, 134
see also institution(s)
sexuality 51, 75, 97, 101–2, 146, 162–3
siblings 44, 51, 60–1, 63, 79
significant other(s) 12, 79–80, 87–8, 112
Siméant, J. 103–4
Simmel, G. 3
social class *see* class
Social Construction of Reality 11–12, 78–83, 117–18, 120, 131
social structures 14–15, 23, 56, 110, 156, 167, 173
sociogenesis 14, 24, 56, 116, 149, 152–3, 159–60, 163, 168
space 1–2, 15–16, 20, 69, 101, 122
  and class 33–6, 38–9, 75
  and gender 35–6, 49
  social space 7, 21–2, 27, 32, 43, 132, 136–7, 142–55, 157, 160–3
  see also neighborhood
spatial socialization *see* space
sport(s) 16, 22, 27, 37, 47–51, 57–8, 68, 97, 111–12, 115, 118–19
Strauss, A. 114, 175 n.7
Streib, J. 28–9, 33, 61–2, 100
Student-Physician (The) 84–6

style(s) 38, 41, 51, 96, 146, 160–2
taste(s) 18, 20, 22–3, 27–8, 37, 46, 49–51, 68, 98–9, 121, 133, 162–5
teachers 9, 13–4, 37, 68, 70–1, 87, 145–6
see also school
time 2, 28–31, 34, 36–9, 49, 59, 62, 73, 75, 98, 113, 121, 131
time period *see* history
transformation 7, 19–20, 88, 100, 114–15, 119, 174–5 n.6
transformative socialization 132–5
see also alternation, conversion, hysteresis, reproduction

Vandebroeck, D. 16, 27

Wacquant, L. 97, 111, 118, 144–5
West, C. 155–7, 161
writing 36, 70–1, 74, 117–20, 133
see also books

Zelizer, V. 35–6
Zerubavel, E. 36, 126–8, 163